T0286924

Money For Tomorrow

Money FOR Tomorrow

HOW TO BUILD AND PROTECT GENERATIONAL WEALTH

Whitney Elkins-Hutten

BiggerPockets® PUBLISHING

Denver, Colorado

Money for Tomorrow: How to Build and Protect Generational Wealth
Whitney Elkins-Hutten

Published by BiggerPockets Publishing, LLC, Denver, CO
Copyright © 2024 by Whitney Elkins-Hutten
All rights reserved.

Publisher's Cataloging-in-Publication Data
Names: Elkins-Hutten, Whitney, author.
Title: Money for tomorrow : how to build and protect generational wealth / Whitney Elkins-Hutten.
Description: Includes bibliographical references. | Denver, CO: BiggerPockets Publishing LLC, 2024.
Identifiers: LCCN: 2023950207 | ISBN: 9781960178121 (hardcover) | 9781960178138 (ebook)
Subjects: LCSH Finance, Personal. | Wealth. | Portfolio management. | Investments. | Investments--Taxation. | BISAC BUSINESS & ECONOMICS / Personal Finance / Money Management | BUSINESS & ECONOMICS / Personal Finance / Retirement Planning | BUSINESS & ECONOMICS / Personal Finance / Investing | BUSINESS & ECONOMICS / Personal Finance / Taxation
Classification: LCC HG179 .E55 2024 | DDC 332.024--dc23

Printed on recycled paper in Canada
MBP 10 9 8 7 6 5 4 3 2 1

DEDICATION

*To Colin and Avery, for always being there
and riding this amazing roller coaster of life with me.*

*Always remember you deserve the world
—you just have to earn it.*

Table of Contents

SECTION I
Building the Foundation for Wealth

SECTION II
Creating Wealth

SECTION III
Keeping Wealth

SECTION IV
Growing Wealth

SECTION V
Passing Wealth On

Note from the Author

Thanks for picking up this book!

Before we dive into the content, I want to make a couple of things clear so you can get the best value out of this book. *Money for Tomorrow* doesn't constitute financial advice, nor is it geared toward in-depth estate planning and tax maneuvers.

Instead, *Money for Tomorrow* is about the fundamental, timeless principles that allow anyone to create and grow wealth. It's a compilation of what I've learned from decades of studying the most successful people—from reading scores of books to attending hundreds of seminars to absorbing countless hours of mentoring from millionaires and billionaires.

You should also know we won't discuss specific paper assets (mutual funds versus stocks versus bonds), specific real estate asset classes (e.g., single-family, multifamily, self-storage, mobile home parks, notes, Opportunity Zones), specialized tax/banking maneuvers, or fancy trust maneuvers like bridge trusts. Why? Because these are all *tactics*. Tactics are useless if you don't understand the fundamentals of how money works and the core principles you need to master to build lasting wealth.

In this book, we will follow the Pareto Principle, or the 80/20 rule. We will discuss how your portfolio is being drained every day without you knowing it; how to assess your individual investment goals, risk, and timelines; how to grow and protect your wealth; and how to pass it on efficiently. The information contained in these pages lays out the core principles of wealth that *anyone* can follow, and will get them 80 percent (or more!) of the way toward their goal of financial freedom. Yes, that includes you!

It is my hope that you enjoy *Money for Tomorrow.*

Introduction

富不过三代
Wealth does not pass three generations.

The ancient Chinese proverb mentioned above is an aphorism, meant to describe the sometimes-inevitable transfer of wealth and power that would happen within dynasties. We've seen it happen time and again—people inherit fortunes, but somehow manage to blow it all within a few decades, or sometimes just a few years.

This economic adage addressing the longevity of multigenerational wealth has been well studied across cultures and professions. Some studies report that 70 percent of affluent people will have lost their wealth by the third generation.[1] It may sound like a myth, but this proverb has been proven true more often than not. Furthermore, it's still applicable today. This trend has also been well documented in famous families, such as the Vanderbilts, Kluges, Hartfords, and Pulitzers, as well as with celebrities like Shia LaBeouf, Michael Jackson, MC Hammer, 50 Cent, Heidi Montag, and Nicolas Cage. You might even know someone like this.

When I first heard that proverb, the question that came to mind was *Why?* Why is it so difficult for people to create wealth and keep it in the family for generations? I decided to do my own research, and what I found was eye-opening.

---

1 "Generational Wealth: Why Do 70% of Families Lose Their Wealth in the 2nd Generation?" Nasdaq, October 19, 2018, https://www.nasdaq.com/articles/generational-wealth%3A-why-do-70-of-families-lose-their-wealth-in-the-2nd-generation-2018-10.

In almost every instance where wealth has disappeared within three generations, financial literacy was the root cause. The truth is that many people simply do not have enough financial education to properly manage their wealth. All the wealth passed on by one generation quickly dissipates due to a variety of reasons: excessive spending, bad debt, bad decisions, poor investments, or simply failing to educate and empower the heirs who inherit their wealth.

We already see this coming to fruition. According to CNBC,[2] baby boomers have more wealth than any other generation, but their millennial children stand to inherit less. Though quite a few factors influence this, the biggest culprit is a lack of knowledge surrounding financial literacy and investments. So much bad information and marketing are disguised as advice and contribute to this problem.

American society conditions us to follow a certain life narrative. We're often told to work hard so we can get a good education and be accepted into college (often at the cost of spending time with family and friends). Once we have a coveted college degree, our next step is to find (and keep) a good job. After that, it's marriage and kids while putting aside a bit of money each month into a retirement account. Hopefully, we have enough saved forty years later that we can spend the last few decades of our life with our family, doing things we actually love.

What a perfect storm waiting to erode your family's wealth. And is that *truly* the American dream?

The fact that you're reading this book tells me that you want more. You're interested in leaving a mark on the world—one that will last for multiple generations. If so, you're in luck. It's not too late, and you're in the right place to learn exactly what you need to create multigenerational wealth that will benefit you and your family for generations to come.

Yes, it sounds like a lot at first. But I promise you that by the end of this book, you'll have the skills you need to make it happen. In fact, you'll start having aha moments within the first few chapters—that's my guarantee to you. How can I be so sure?

Well, just a few years ago, I was exactly where you are now—thinking that once you make more money, once you close the next deal, you'll be able to solve your problems. You see, as an investor, even though I was closing hundreds of thousands of dollars in deals each year, I still felt

---

2 Jessica Dickler, "Booms have more wealth 'than any other generation,' but millenials may not inherit as much as they hope," CNBC, Dec 9, 2022, https://www.cnbc.com/2022/12/09/great-wealth-transfer-why-millennials-may-inherit-less-than-expected.html.

broke. If you've ever felt similarly, know that you're not crazy—in fact, this is a common feeling I've heard my clients talk about.

Does any of this seem familiar to you?

- I make good money at my job, but I feel broke.
- I think about my finances all the time, more than I would like to.
- I am afraid to overhaul my finances; I don't even want to look at them.
- I don't have clarity on my financial goals, which makes me feel insecure.
- My partner and I fight over money regularly.
- I hate talking about finances; I would rather just do deals.

These feelings are completely normal and more common than you'd think. You shouldn't feel ashamed for feeling this way either. Know that you are in good company, and I hope to help you reduce (and maybe even eliminate!) those fears. It's difficult to master generational wealth—and experience the joys of investing—with these fears hanging over you.

Think of this process as a grand board game. It's the multigenerational wealth game, and your winning hinges on understanding your objectives, the rules of play, and how to find your success.

1. The first step involves knowing your objective. You need to determine the type of life you want to live and how you want to use passive income.
2. Once you have your objective in mind, you shift to learning the rules of the wealth-building game. This book is broken up into four sections, which function as the pillars for your multigenerational wealth strategy. Each pillar provides a rule you can use to achieve your objective.
3. Last, you'll learn how to play the game successfully. With clear objectives and rules in mind, you'll be able to make tactical plays on the game board. These are your financial decisions, investments, and wealth-management techniques that will take you from financial stability to financial prosperity that will last generations!

Throughout the book, I will demonstrate these three concepts, which I've learned through hard work and trial and error. The skills I have acquired and the knowledge I have gained allow me to create wealth beyond my wildest dreams. I've created a foundation for my family's future, my daughter's future, and generations beyond. These very same principles I live my investing life by are the same principles I teach my clients through my Investor Accelerator Program at AshWealth.com. I'm excited to share them with you throughout this book.

It is my hope that you will enjoy this book as we explore how to find your objective, the rules of the multigenerational wealth game, and determine how to measure and build success. My true wish is that you go beyond this enjoyment and apply the principles laid out for you to change the trajectory of your life and create a secure future for your family for generations to come.

When you master the multigenerational wealth game, you will be an unstoppable investor (real estate or otherwise), intrapreneur, entrepreneur, partner, and family member. At the end of the day, isn't that why we do what we do? To be the best version of ourselves for those that we love and value? You owe it to yourself and to the people you love. Let's get started!

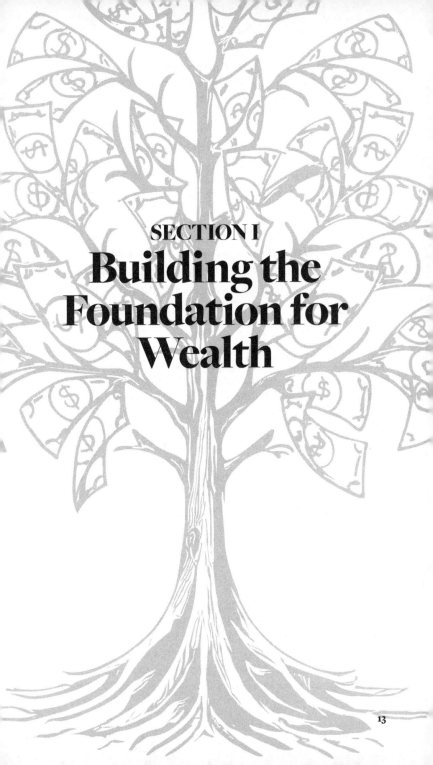

SECTION I
Building the Foundation for Wealth

CHAPTER 1

What Wealth Really Means

'Financial freedom' is not a dirty statement.
It means your lifestyle is paid for and you can
focus on what you were put on this earth to do.

When I am introduced on stage at speaking events, the audience hears that I am a partner in more than $800 million worth of real estate, including over 6,500 multifamily units, 2,200-plus self-storage units, a dozen car washes, and more. I would imagine if I were in the audience's seat, those numbers would sound impressive. But my immediate next thought would be, *How on earth can I replicate that?*

I'll let you in on a little secret: When I started my wealth journey, I didn't have a plan, nor did I know the rules of wealth building. Looking back, I really didn't know anything—I wish I had a playbook like this to help me get started! What I did have was a strong desire to figure it out. I knew it would be up to me to make it happen. Fast-forward to today, and where I am now is the result of many years of work and many lessons learned the hard way.

How My Wealth Journey Began
It all started in 2002. my relationship had burned to the ground. I had been left with a mortgage payment on a house I couldn't afford and no idea how I was going to make the payments each month. In addition, the house needed a full gut rehab in order to sell. I was in dire straits, but I came up with a plan: I was going to complete the rehab myself.

I stuffed the house full of roommates and did DIY renovations by getting my friends to help me and paying them in sushi, beer, and pizza. Sure, it was hard. YouTube didn't exist back then. However, Home Depot did. I bought their *Home Improvement 1-2-3* book to learn how to do all the renovations on my own. But it was rewarding work.

Eleven months later, I sold the property. I was relieved the house was off my hands, but after the dust settled and the check cleared, a light bulb went off in my head.

Not only did I manage to sell the house, but I *made a significant profit on it.* Because I had roommates, my living expenses were covered in full— mortgage, utilities, everything. I actually had extra money each month. In fact, I made more money on that single transaction than I was earning per year at my day job, which had me often traveling eighty hours per week. And I eliminated my personal living expenses in the process.

That first foray into real estate lit a fire in me I've been kindling ever since. However, I got my first reality check early. My second live-in flip didn't go as well. I did everything I wasn't supposed to do in real estate and managed to break even on it just before the financial crisis that started in 2008.

That didn't stop me. I knew that there was money to be made and that flipping real estate could be wildly profitable. So, my husband and I started doing just that—moving into properties that needed a little TLC, renovating them while we lived there, and then selling them for a profit. We're a great team, and over the next ten years, we went on to flip over $5 million in residential real estate.

But despite this, I knew something was a little off. After we sold a house, we had to be on the prowl for the next one. If we didn't keep flipping, we could run out of money. We were pros at creating equity, but we lacked monthly reliable cash flow to feel confident enough to step away from our W-2 jobs. Even though we were moving in the right direction and building our net worth, we were still shackled by the golden handcuffs of paycheck dependence. We had more money, but our financial situation wasn't where we wanted it to be.

After *years* of house hacking, rehabbing, then selling properties, a casual conversation with a friend gave me an aha moment. My friend's million-dollar question was: "Why don't you put a tenant in it?" I know it may seem like an obvious point, but I had never thought of it. My friend was right. Plus, I had housed tenants before, in my very first flip. I just didn't see my roommates as tenants because I was living there with them.

My husband and I shifted our business model. We started flipping properties outside of our home. But instead of selling them, we turned them into rental units. The rent from each property covered the mortgage and expenses related to the home, and the extra money created a healthy cash flow for us. With reliable monthly income coming in, plus the new value of the property after renovation, we were able to refinance out most of the money we spent on the project to invest in new deals—the BRRRR strategy. Our cash flow situation really changed, and we were able to hold on to the property equity and increase our net worth.

We were on the right path—after all, our financial situation was a far cry from what it was when we first started. But it was still hard for us to hold on to our wealth. Sure, money makes you rich, but it's what you do with that money that makes you *wealthy*.

On top of that, the business ate into our time, and even though our rentals were profitable, scaling them was difficult. We worked *in* the business as much as *on* it. Even though we worked with property managers to complete the work, I was still balancing loans, bookkeeping, making construction decisions, as well as finding and underwriting the next deal.

What's the point of having money if you can't enrich your life and the lives of those around you? We were again losing our time freedom at an alarming rate. I kept thinking to myself that there had to be another way.

When I Started Thinking About Multigenerational Wealth

As the years went by and our family started to grow, the idea of *passing our wealth on* started to become more of a priority to me. I wanted to create a solid foundation that would support us and the next generation of our family. I didn't come from a family who laid a foundation for me. Money wasn't something we discussed, and I didn't even know what financial literacy was until I went in search of it as an adult in my thirties. I wanted to be different from the way I was raised.

That's why I wanted to write this book—to share my story and what I've learned about building generational wealth.

Hope isn't a plan. If you don't have a plan for your time and money, someone else will—and I can promise you that it won't end up being half as good as what you could've come up with on your own. Not having a plan is especially hard on the family members you left behind. In my immediate family alone, three estates have gone through probate and two estates have been passed along through trusts. Note the word "estate" doesn't mean it actually has money! As a matter of fact, those combined five estates lost over $700,000 in potential wealth transfer to my generation alone. Ninety-five percent of that money could have been saved with simple financial education and planning.

Now, I know what you're thinking: *Whitney, you co-own thousands of properties. Is having an additional $700,000 really that important to you?* Yes, it is. Because the real issue arises when you look at the potential growth and compounding of that money over time. That $700,000, compounded at 7 percent over 30 years, is a $5.3 million net loss to my family's future wealth plan. A loss that simply didn't have to happen.

My situation isn't unique. This happens to countless families every single year. Almost everyone in my personal network has experienced something like this, and I can confidently guess that you have too.

And that, dear reader, is what this book is about. It's about understanding the principles that will help you execute the four phases of multigenerational wealth: creating wealth, keeping wealth, investing wealth, and passing on wealth.

Of course, this all comes with a disclaimer: This book is not meant to offer financial, legal, or tax advice, and I would strongly suggest consulting with your professional team before making any major decisions. (Creating a solid team of professionals is one of the things we touch on in this book as well.) These are the things I've learned along the way— through experience and learning from thousands of hours of books, podcasts, workshops, seminars, and paid coaching.

I've set out to consolidate and simplify the principles into a workable plan, so you have a guide that you can consult as you take on this rewarding challenge. They say that the shortest distance between two points is a straight line. But what if you're able to fold the paper in half and connect those two dots, essentially collapsing time? That's what this book does. It collapses all the steps for you, saving you time so you don't have to do it all on your own.

The principles contained herein have been around for millennia. They work now and will continue to work. They ignore inflation and recessions and can be applied in any economy around the world. I think of it like trying to find the exit in a dark room that's filled with obstacles. If you flip a light switch, you'll be able to see exactly where to go without stubbing your toe or crashing into something that could hurt you.

This book is your proverbial light switch. Once illuminated, you'll be able to thread together the perfect path for you, one that will secure your future, the future of your family, and bring you true freedom.

Personal Symbols of Wealth

What was a symbol of wealth to you when you were growing up? For me, the symbols were having a pool, fancy cars, lots of cool toys and gadgets, and designer clothes; traveling out of the country; and going to an elite private school. I've had this conversation with so many of my clients, and the answers changed depending on who I asked. I've heard: living in a two-story house, owning a cell phone (this was before they became an extension of our bodies), and being able to take vacation abroad every year.

You probably don't still have those same views on wealth you had as a kid. The true definition of wealth will vary based on what you value as an individual. And that's the very first step in creating a foundation for multigenerational wealth: figuring out what being "wealthy" means to you.

The national conversations on wealth are changing. "Financial freedom," for example, is a concept popularized by the FIRE (Financial Independence, Retire Early) community. It's based on the idea of achieving positive cash flow from investments so you can retire early.

On the face of it, the FIRE concept seems fulfilling enough. But in my opinion, it leaves a lot to be desired. There isn't much emphasis on building a legacy, and you're often limited by what you can do after early retirement because the focus is on investing only to keep up with inflation, not to create multigenerational wealth. For example, you might have to move to a different part of the country where the cost of living is lower if you want to be able to retire early on your investments, or even have to cut back on your spending if the market experiences a downturn, lowering the amount of money you make from your investments over a particular time period. Once you get down to the nitty-gritty, FIRE leaves a bitter taste in your mouth.

That's why I want to help you understand what true wealth really means, so you can create the foundation on which you'll build your legacy. True wealth all boils down to freedom, and more specifically, freedom in five ways.

1. Financial freedom
2. Time freedom
3. Location freedom
4. Choice freedom
5. Impact freedom

Financial Freedom

I've always considered financial freedom not as a goal to aspire to, but more of a state of being. It's when you have enough money coming in from your assets to cover the lifestyle you want to have *without having to ever go to work*. It involves:

1. Getting out of debt so you can live without worrying about bills.
2. Having enough money to pay for the lifestyle you desire (not the lifestyle you are currently living) and still putting money aside for a rainy day.
3. Investing in assets (businesses, notes, and real estate), as opposed to liabilities, that build wealth and provide future financial security.

Planning for the future is key, as is creating healthy habits that support your goals. I've put it first on the list because it's the first goalpost on the way to building wealth. Once achieved, financial freedom allows you to be more free in the other areas of time, location, choice, and impact.

Time Freedom

If you've ever felt the strain of sticking to a specific schedule for work, day in and day out and regardless of the weather, then time freedom might appeal to you. Time freedom gives you the luxury of spending your day however you choose. This could include taking some days off work to enjoy hobbies or going on spontaneous trips with no worry of having to get back by a specific date. Heck, it could be not working at all!

Arguably one of the best parts of time freedom is the control you have over how your days are spent, allowing for more diverse experiences and the potential for greater personal growth. Time freedom means you can prioritize family, leisure, and self-care without sacrificing career success or goals.

Location Freedom

Location freedom is popular, especially with the rise of digital nomads. In its simplest form, location freedom is the ability to work from anywhere. That might conjure up images of typing away on your laptop on a beach in Thailand while you sip from a coconut, but that's not the only, or even the best, definition. Location freedom can mean living a nomadic lifestyle, relocating permanently to a different country, or anything in between. The key is having the flexibility to choose where you want to live and work without being tied down to one place.

When I talk about location freedom, I mean being able to live any-where in the world because you've created such a solid foundation for wealth that your business and investments can run themselves without you being tied to a physical location. That sounds like *true* freedom to me.

Choice Freedom

Have you ever been presented with an opportunity but found yourself thinking, "If only I didn't have to do _____, then I could do this?" If you answered yes to this, then choice freedom is one of the most attractive advantages of creating multigenerational wealth. Think about it: Would you make the same choices you do now if you had financial freedom?

After achieving financial freedom, you'll find that it's much easier to make choices that will bring you enjoyment and help propel you toward your own unique goals instead of feeling beholden to a certain path. This is what I call choice freedom.

You're able to make your own decisions that best fit your values and desires. You know that no matter what choice you make, it won't have any long-term financial implications for you or your family. This par-ticular aspect might not be glamorous—it could be as simple as being able to sleep in on a Monday morning—but it's invaluable to creating true wealth.

Impact Freedom

Of the five freedoms, impact freedom comes with the most nuance. Describing impact freedom is like saying you have the freedom to make an impact in your community. Maybe you have never thought of having the freedom to make an impact. I hadn't! But for me, it was the missing link of my journey and THE reason I'm writing this book for you.

More than just being able to make your own choices, and have control over your time and location, you can invest your energy into meaningful causes that are important to you. You are able to use your resources and talents to not only better yourself, but also make an impact on the lives of others. A whole new world of possibilities opens up.

And isn't that one of the reasons why we all want to create genera-tional wealth? Leaving a real legacy behind involves making a lasting impression on our community, and on the greater world.

You see, these five freedoms give us the chance to do more than just accumulate money; they give us an opportunity to share our power with those who might need it the most, even if we don't know them personally. Furthermore, impact starts at home. If you can invest in yourself, how many people could you impact? If you invest in your family and kids, then you're amplifying your impact exponentially. This goes both ways—positively *and* negatively. The whole concept of impact freedom can be summed up in one popular quote by Mahatma Gandhi: "Be the change you want to see in the world."

The five freedoms of money, choice, location, time, and impact form the foundation of a true multigenerational wealth plan. Throughout the pages of this book, I'll give you more insight into how you can achieve each of these, regardless of where you're starting right now.

How can I be so sure that I can help you? There's a science behind creating wealth. While every path might not be the same, they all need to be built on the same foundation. I'll be sharing those timeless principles with you. Are you ready to get started?

═══ YOUR CHAPTER ACTION PLAN ═══

1. Write down which of the five freedoms you desire to have in life.
2. Rate on a scale of 0–10 where you are with achieving that desired freedom (10 being you have achieved that freedom).
   - Financial freedom
   - Time freedom
   - Location freedom
   - Choice freedom
   - Impact freedom
3. Pick the top two freedoms you want to make serious progress toward in the next five years.

CHAPTER 2

How Your Mindset Impacts Your Goals (And the Traps We All Fall Prey To)

When you change your internal conversation from 'I can't' to 'How can I?' your world will change in the blink of an eye.

If you read the first chapter of this book and felt like the five freedoms aren't possible for you, put that thought as far away from your mind as possible—at least for the remainder of this chapter. You see, it's never too late to make changes.

When I first started my real estate business, I constantly felt like I was playing catch-up. I wondered why I didn't discover this when I was a teenager, or even before I turned 25. As I rubbed shoulders with other investors and even taught this framework to my clients (some of them older than me), I realized that it's never too late to make changes that can positively alter the trajectory of your life and those around you.

Why is that? Because the principles for creating wealth don't discriminate. Your age, background, culture—none of that matters. Creating a stable wealth foundation follows a predictable pattern. A formula, if you will.

It all boils down to a four-pronged approach: creating wealth, keeping wealth, growing wealth, and then passing it on. This book has been divided into each part of that approach. Before we get to that, though, we're going to discuss the first steps to wealth creation, the very first things you need to do before you even start thinking about creating wealth.

You need a system for choosing the right goals and achieving them. It's critical to wealth creation. Without a system, you may spend your time bouncing from one goal to the next without ever making any real progress. Or you might make bad decisions because of how it feels in the moment, instead of focusing on long-term strategy. A good system can help you differentiate between wants and needs, prioritize objectives, and hold yourself accountable for results. It challenges you to take an honest assessment of your current situation and stay true to the plan you put in place.

You might become overwhelmed by the bigger picture. Or you might find yourself distracted by the day-to-day tasks required. After all, you're creating something that will potentially span generations. If you have a family, the decisions you make today will help your great-grandchildren live better lives. It's a lot to plan for.

Fortunately, you don't have to figure out what to do on your own! Remember how I mentioned that wealth creation is a science? The framework stays the same. It's the very one I learned from my mentors that helped me to get to over $800 million in assets in partnership and the one I teach to my coaching clients.

It all boils down to two key things: your mindset and how you break down your goals.

The Importance of Mindset

Before I figured out how to take control of my mindset, I had difficulty achieving my goals. I found myself lagging behind where I wanted to be and unsure of where to go next. As I started to shift my mindset, though, I started to see results.

The importance of mindset—how you think and feel, and what those thoughts and feelings influence you to do—isn't talked about enough in the context of generational wealth.

For starters, the average person interested in wealth creation typically has a fixed mindset. Their goal hinges on getting to a specific income or net worth by a specific point in time. Some people are so focused on that goal they run away from their current reality. Or worse, they may come from a place of scarcity and think that everyone is out to get them.

That's not a fun life to live.

I used to think like that too. Initially, I thought I was going to forever be an employee, but then I stumbled into flipping houses. Even though I was leveling up my income, I hadn't upgraded my mindset. When my husband and I were flipping houses, we obsessed over finding the next gem. After we closed one deal, I always challenged myself to find another property more profitable than the last, rather than finding better and higher use of our funds to grow and amplify our wealth. My thoughts were linear, and I was fixed on a singular, specific path unable to see that there was a whole world of endless possibilities to grow my wealth and leverage my time.

My life changed when I began adopting a growth mindset. I embraced my views, intelligence, abilities, and talents as learnable and capable of improvement through effort. When I ran into an obstacle where I before would say, "I can't," I began asking better questions like "How can I?" I started to see abundance all around me, and because I was working hard to change myself, my world started *conspiring for* me with opportunities.

While a fixed mindset will certainly get you *somewhere*, it usually won't get you to where you want to be. Once you get into the mindset of seeing everything as a growth opportunity and looking for ways to transform your current life, it will be easier to create goals that will take you closer to creating generational wealth. Being able to transition from flipping houses to holding on to them and renting them was a by-product of a growth mindset.

If you look at every moment as an opportunity for growth, you'll find that the dots connect much easier, and you'll be able to thread together a path that saves you time and resources in the pursuit of multigenerational wealth.

The Importance of Breaking Down Your Goals

One of my favorite quotes is from Thomas Carlyle and goes something like this: "A man without a goal is like a ship without a rudder." Goal setting is the key to unlocking the life you dream of.

This chapter will help you do more than set goals. I'm going to arm you with the knowledge necessary to *achieve* what you set out to do—by figuring out what you want, why you want it, and who you have to become to make it happen. This secret framework is an advanced goal-setting system that will simplify the entire process.

The Three Most Powerful Questions You Must Ask to Achieve Your Goals

Question 1: *What do you want?*

If you were to write down some of your life goals right now, what would they look like? Maybe you would write things like:

- I don't want to sit in a cubicle for sixty hours per week and not get to spend time with my family.
- I don't want to be stressed out about money and neck-deep in debt.
- I don't want to have to cut my vacation short for work.
- I don't want to have to shop from the clearance rack.

While those are admirable things, they're not exactly *goals* because you're not detailing what you want to happen. Instead, you're listing out the things you *don't* want to happen. That can make your whole plan ineffective because creating multigenerational wealth relies on specificity.

You must be specific. Saying you don't want to sit in a cubicle for sixty hours a week can mean sitting in a cubicle for *forty* hours a week. And that isn't what we want either. But if you set a goal to be able to work from anywhere with a consistent cash flow coming in, suddenly the conversation changes and you can start creating a path and plan forward—one that will get you there.

That's why I want to introduce you to this advanced goal-setting system that I learned from Gary W. Keller and Jay Papasan's book, *The ONE Thing.* The concept is rooted in defining what you *really* want in life. We'll figure this out in three key steps. The first step will help you to figure out what you want by exploring the answers to three pivotal questions.

- What do you want your life to look like financially in five years?
- Where do you need to be in one year to be on track for your five-year plan?
- Where are you right now?

Finding the answers to those three questions is going to require a lot of honesty from you, so give yourself ten minutes (or more!) to think about the answers to the questions above. Don't be afraid to use dollar figures to describe your wants. I'd even suggest writing the answers down, so you have a paper trail going forward.

You might not like what you discover—especially when it's time to think about the last question—but uncovering all those feelings and taking an honest, no-nonsense look at your life is imperative to setting the foundation for your future success.

Question 2: Why do you want it?

Once you've got the (honest) answers to the above three questions, we can move on to the second part of the goal-setting framework, which revolves around figuring out why you want what you do.

For example, if you answered the previous three questions to say that you want to have $10,000 per month in passive income—that's superficial. Money on its own is pointless, as it only gains value once it is spent or put to work for you. So, in this second step, I want you to focus on your *why* … your *real* why.

Your goal needs to impact you on a deep, emotional level. That's the only way it will be able to motivate you. You need to have such a visceral reaction to what you want that it gets you out of bed in the morning and shines like a glimmering beacon.

Having a worthwhile goal will make the steps in this book more manageable. Your goal will push you forward when things get difficult. Additionally, your *why* will become your North Star. It will be the gut feeling that will help you decide which investments are the best fit for you, or the kind of business you should build. It has to light a fire under you or else this whole plan will crumble before you get started. Needing more money to pay bills isn't rewarding, but getting your time back to create experiences with your children before they leave the house for school every morning is *very* motivating.

Fortunately, I have an exercise that will make it easier to figure out your *why* and help you uncover the real, emotional reason for your goal. I call it the Seven Layers of Why, a concept I learned from Tony Robbins at Unleash the Power Within.[3] It's best explained with an example, so I'll show you how to do it by using the goal of earning $10,000 passively per month.

1. Why do you want to earn $10,000 per month? Answer: *Because I want to earn more money.*
2. Why do you want to earn more money? Answer: *Because I want to be able to pay off my debt.*
3. Why do you want to be able to pay off your debt? Answer: *I want to be able to buy income-earning assets.*

---

3   Tony Robbins, "Unleash the Power Within," 2021, virtual seminar.

4. Why do you want to buy income-earning assets? Answer: *With income coming in, I will be able to work less.*
5. Why do you want to be able to work less? Answer: *I love traveling and want to be able to travel more.*
6. Why do you want to be able to travel more? Answer: *So I can spend more time with my kids and teach them about the world.*
7. Why do you want to spend more time with your kids and teach them about the world? Answer: *I want the freedom to spend my time however I want to.*

I want you to spend a few minutes and take yourself through this exercise. Write down your process. When you do, you'll realize that your real *why* might not be so different from the one I listed above. I've seen it time and again: When I share this method with my friends and clients, almost everyone's *why* is having one of the five freedoms we discussed in Chapter 1, the most common being the freedom of time or choice.

Still, it's important to do this exercise so you can gain a true and deep understanding of what it is you want.

For example, after doing the Seven Layers of Why, I figured out that freedom to choose is most important to me. Knowing that about myself has helped me choose the right investments, including moving away from the time suck of flipping houses I started with all those years ago.

When you have your *why* in mind, obstacles don't feel like insurmountable challenges. Instead of feeling overwhelmed or discouraged, you're motivated because you recognize it for what it really is—a stepping stone to helping you get what you truly want.

Question 3: Who do you have to become to get it?
Once you've finished the second step, we can move on to the third and final part of this advanced goal-setting framework. Now that you understand what you want, and why you truly want it, it's time to explore *who you have to become to get what you want.*

That's the final piece of the puzzle—figuring out the mindset, the skills, and the kind of network you need to cultivate to achieve your goal. This part takes the most time (outside of putting in the work, of course), but it is immensely important to setting yourself up for success.

Are you ready?

Let's start by tackling the saboteurs and traps to look out for that can sidetrack you before you even get started.

The Saboteurs

If it were easy, everyone would do it. The road to creating the life you want for yourself and your family will be paved with challenges.

There's a silver lining, though. The challenges you face won't be unique to you. In fact, they'll be largely the same for everyone, just packaged in different ways. Tony Robbins in his Unleash the Power Within[4] intensive calls them "saboteurs," or the reasons why you could possibly fail in your financial plan. There's always a reason why you may fail, but being able to anticipate it gives you the best chance of success.

What are these saboteurs? In my experience, there are ten of them—different personality traits or mindsets that make it difficult for us to get to the next level. They are like little devils sitting on your shoulder, whispering limiting beliefs into your ear.

We often pick up these saboteurs from our surroundings, whether parents, friends, or teachers. Knowing what they are is the first step to being able to overcome them as quickly as possible. Look at the list below and think about your own mindset.

Have you fallen victim to any (or several) of these saboteurs?

The Judge

The Judge beats down any idea. They focus on the negative before the positive, and point out all the bad things in any given plan. Left unchecked, The Judge will ruin a plan before it gets off the ground.

The Victim

The Victim is at the mercy of their circumstances. They moan about what's happening in their life without any action to fix it. The Victim will be very reactionary instead of proactive.

It's true that you can be *victimized*. Bad things happen to everyone. However, if you constantly think, feel, or react like you're at the mercy of your circumstances, that can become a saboteur. How you react to the bad stuff is what makes the difference.

The Pleaser

This is one of the most common saboteurs. The Pleaser is always trying to take care of everyone, making sure that everybody in the room is okay. They forget to work on their own goals, dreams, and priorities, and are instead concerned about everyone else.

---

4 Robbins, "Unleash the Power Within."

The Avoider
This one synergizes well with The Pleaser for all the wrong reasons. The Avoider doesn't want to do the work for whatever reason—maybe it's too hard, maybe they must learn something new, or maybe they just don't know how to figure it out. They don't want to experience the growing pains that come with trying new things.

The Perfectionist (or Stickler)
The Perfectionist needs everything to be perfect, to the detriment of a project. I am a recovering Perfectionist. For me, things had to be immensely perfect before I could move forward with a plan. In my case, it was extreme. For example, if I was recording a video of me speaking and I said "ah" or "um," I would delete the footage and rerecord the entire thing, from the *beginning*. As you can imagine, that saboteur didn't play well with the goals I had for myself, as nothing is ever perfect. If you wait for perfection, you'll never launch.

The W"restless"r
In pursuit of your goals, the path won't always be crystal clear. The W"restless"r finds it hard to sit in the ambiguity of a situation, even if it might end up working out the way they think. They're similar to The Perfectionist saboteur in that they feel uncomfortable if they aren't *doing* something. More often than you think, patience is part of the process.

The Controller
Have you ever heard someone say, "If I need something done well, I have to do it myself?" Chances are, that person is a Controller. This saboteur wants to own every single decision, resist help from more knowledgeable people, and even resist working in a team or collaborating with others.

The Hyper-Achiever
The Hyper-Achiever is obsessed with setting and achieving goals—and as soon as they hit one milestone, they're making plans for another. Setting and achieving goals is good, but for The Hyper-Achiever, it's an empty, soul-sucking process based on comparison that might cause them more harm than good in the long run. If you were a straight-A student in school, there's a chance that you're still dealing with this saboteur even to this day.

The Hyper-Rational

The Hyper-Rational saboteur talks themself out of anything and everything using data and details. They're going to blame their inability to move forward on being rational instead of identifying what it really is: a fear of taking risks. Anything that we do—whether it's the journey you choose to take or an investment—has some risk involved. If you talk yourself out of everything, you'll never achieve your goal.

The Hyper-Vigilant

This is just a very nice word for a micromanager. There's an element of control to it, kind of like The Controller, but The Hyper-Vigilant micromanages everything down to the minutia without taking the chance to focus on the big picture. This saboteur gets stuck in the detail and ends up working *in* the business, not *on* the business.

Now that we've covered these ten saboteurs, I want you to take a moment to see if you can see yourself in any of these self-sabotaging habits. We all have them, and it's not an indictment on your ability to be successful if you find yourself with one, two, three, or even all ten of these thinking patterns.

This exercise isn't about judging yourself. Instead, it's about understanding your blind sides so that when any of these saboteurs pop up, you can recognize them for what they are and not let them derail you from your goal.

Eight Traps That Can Cause Failure

Being able to recognize your saboteur is imperative to your journey, but there's something else that can pop up in tandem with a saboteur that can make it harder for you to achieve your goals. I like to call these "traps," another concept I learned from Tony Robbins at his Unleash the Power Within[5] seminar. Unlike saboteurs, they are deceptive real-life situations that can ensnare you if you aren't careful.

Traps are more insidious than a saboteur; sometimes you won't even realize you've been caught in one until you stop to consider what's actually going on in your life. Let's take a look at the eight traps that, without proper intervention, can lead to failure.

---

5 Robbins, "Unleash the Power Within."

Failing to take ownership of your life

We all know people like this—everything is everybody else's fault, and they never want to take ownership of the direction of their lives. If they miss out on a job promotion, it's the manager's fault for playing favorites; if they cause a car accident, it's the other person's fault for not paying attention.

People like these are often unhappy with where they are in life and have chosen to listen to The Victim instead of making a change in their life. It's when we take extreme ownership of our lives—owning our failures and obstacles—that we are able to move forward because we're back in control. Challenges will arise, but it's our responses to those challenges that make us who we are.

Avoiding responsibility or culpability

People who avoid responsibility or culpability blame everyone else for their actions, and will go to extreme lengths to avoid being held responsible. When something bad happens, they refuse to consider what they could have done differently to avoid the situation, and instead place all the blame on someone else.

Taking responsibility lets you take agency in your life. By doing so, you're allowing yourself the ability to move past difficult situations with confidence instead of a condescending tone.

Focusing on why something isn't possible

This trap is subtle. It utilizes a fixed mindset and even channels some aspects of The Hyper-Rational saboteur. Many people discourage themselves before they even get started by focusing on all the things that *could* go wrong, and all the reasons why something isn't possible.

Much of what you have achieved and will go on to achieve stems from what you believe is possible. Your brain has an uncanny ability to help you make the choices and find the solutions that will get you closer to your big goal—*but only if you actually think it can happen.* If you focus on the negative side of things, you'll always end up with negative results.

Failing to find a yes

This trap goes hand in hand with The Judge saboteur. You end up never saying yes to anything because you're focused on the negative side of things, or you trash every idea that comes your way without fully understanding it and exploring the possibilities.

Failing to find a yes could be the reason you don't start on projects that could be financially beneficial or fun for you. When you decide to find your yes, you open yourself up to a world of possibilities. Even saying yes to brainstorming can be fruitful to ideas you might be hesitant about.

Attributing agency to difficulty

Agency is one of the foundational concepts that will set you up for success—choosing to own all your freedoms (financial, time, location, choice, and impact). This trap involves choosing difficulty instead of agency—for example, focusing on all the obstacles that could be associated with making the BIG choice of choosing freedom instead of shifting to a growth mindset.

On the other hand, when you choose to have agency, you suddenly have a voice. You're able to make firm decisions and start pursuing the five freedoms intensely. No longer are you caught being reactionary. Instead, you show firm conviction in your hopes and dreams.

Accepting your psychological immune system

This trap is another common, insidious one that many people fall victim to without realizing it. We've been conditioned by society to think that as we get older, the way we are is the way we will always be. Yet as children, growth comes naturally. Every day feels like a new adventure, and it's universally accepted that the way you are today as a kid will not be who you are when you become an adult.

As adults, we lose that spark. Instead of continuing to dream about our futures and thinking about who we will be next, we start to believe that we're "all done growing." This trap is like a death knell to your dreams. Your psychological immune system isn't set in stone. You can become the person needed to make your dreams a reality—regardless of your age, where you are now, or what you may think about yourself right now.

Basing your self-esteem on being right

We've all met someone like this, whether it's at work or at parties, or it might be someone in your family. Their opinion on a topic or their answer to a question is *always* the correct one. Even if they're just repeating your idea, they need to do it or else they just won't feel comfortable. People like this have built their entire personality on being right. It's as important to them as oxygen. They refuse to acknowledge that they could be wrong about something because if they're wrong, their whole world would crumble.

When you admit that you can be wrong, you are able to start to grow. This growth allows you to take on new projects, make mistakes, and learn from them.

Lacking self-awareness

This entire chapter is focused on being able to hold up a mirror to ourselves and isolate the self-sabotaging behaviors that we're engaged in right now. A lack of self-awareness is possibly the biggest trap there is. Without self-awareness, you won't even realize that you have a saboteur or that you're caught in a trap that can cause failure.

Take a sticky note and write down the saboteurs and traps that might be making it difficult for you to grow, and stick it somewhere you will see it every day. Or you can write them down in your journal. Whatever you do, you need to put them somewhere that will remind you of these points of negativity. The purpose of this exercise is to learn to catch yourself when you're thinking negatively about a project.

That way, whenever you hit a roadblock, a challenging situation, or any point where you just want to give up, you can be reminded which saboteur or trap is showing up for you at that moment so you can isolate it, deal with it, and then move past it toward success.

═══ YOUR CHAPTER ACTION PLAN ═══

1. Answer the three advanced goal-setting questions.
   - What do you want?
   - Why do you want it? Don't forget to go seven layers deep!
   - Who do you have to become to get it?
     - **Mindset:** Where are you in a fixed mindset? Where do you need to cultivate a growth mindset?
     - **Skills**
     - **Networks**
2. Review the list of ten saboteurs. Which ones are you most prone to? (Psst ... everyone has at least one!)
3. Review the eight traps. Which ones are you most prone to? (Again, everyone has at least one!)

Real Stories of Money for Tomorrow
PRINCIPLES IN ACTION

Teaching Your Kids About Money—Maya Corbic, CPA, @teach.kids.money, and founder and CEO, Dinarii Financial Education Academy

Don't save what money is left after spending. Rather, only spend the money that remains after saving funds.
—WARREN BUFFETT

Growing up, I didn't exactly receive a crash course in the topic of money. I learned a lot by observing. My parents were good at budgeting and saving money, but did not invest or even have credit cards. So, when it came to financial literacy, I had to be my own guide. Turns out, wealth creation is a whole different ball game than budgeting, paying bills, and saving up.

This is why I capitalize on real-life opportunities where I get to teach my children various money lessons. One particular event comes to mind that helped my kids learn how to be money savvy.

It happened when they were thirteen and fifteen years old. It was summer, and my next-door neighbor's grass was knee-high. Some of the other folks in the neighborhood were fuming and even considering calling in the cavalry (aka the city). Drama alert! But I had a better plan up my sleeve—one that would not only solve the grassy predicament, but also teach my kids some invaluable money lessons.

At the time, my youngsters didn't have part-time jobs and were itching to earn some cash. So, I told them that moneymaking opportunities were all around—they just had to spot them. I did not realize this was also going to be a source of a lot of hate on social media, but more on that later.

We put a plan in place for how they were going to approach our neighbor and pitch him their top-notch lawn-mowing service.

First, I helped them research how much lawn-mowing services cost in our area. The rates were anywhere from $30 to $40 per property. I told them to ask for $40 per visit and be ready to negotiate. We role-played some negotiation scenarios.

Now, negotiation is a skill I never really mastered. Unfortunately, my lack of negotiation prowess meant missed opportunities in the corporate world. But not for my little grass-cutting prodigies! I wanted them to embrace the art of haggling and never settle for the first price thrown their way.

Marketing and sales are skills that never made it into my curriculum growing up, but I am determined to teach my children. I taught the kids that storytelling is a powerful tool that elicits generosity and support from others. Together, we crafted a compelling script that showcased their aspirations of saving up for a laptop. Now, who wouldn't want to support a couple of enterprising kids working their way toward tech glory?

It was intimidating for the kids to talk to our neighbor on their own. They were nervous. But I firmly believe in fostering their independence and social skills, so off they went, offering their deal. And guess what? They nailed it! Talk about proud parent moments.

The lessons did not stop there. They continued well after the grass had been trimmed and the sweaty brows had been wiped. We had a rule that they needed to save 50 percent of everything they earned, and once their savings accumulated, we invested the money. The remaining 50 percent was for donating and spending. The kids decided how that should be split.

Now, life has a funny way of sneaking in some lessons when you least expect them. And my kids got a taste of that reality. Turns out, they forgot to collect payment right after finishing a job and failed to keep track of the number of services they had completed. When payment time arrived, there was a discrepancy between what they thought was owed and what our neighbor believed. This was an important lesson in invoicing and recordkeeping, and I bought them a cheap invoice book.

Another challenge they faced was what to do with their budding lawn-mowing business when we went on vacation. They had to find a reliable friend to substitute for them. I explained that they could pay their friend the full $40 per visit, or they could negotiate a lower amount and keep the difference for themselves since they had secured the gig. They chose to pay their friend the full amount, which was admirable.

I was quite pleased with the lessons they were learning from this experience, and I decided to share them on my Instagram account (@teach.kids.money), where I got many positive comments but also got slammed with some mean-spirited ones.

As it took the kids about an hour to mow that property, they were making $40 per hour. That was more money per hour than what some of their teen friends were making as cashiers, kitchen help, etc. Some of the hateful comments were stating that I was disrespectful and teaching my kids to demean minimum-wage jobs.

I do not see it that way. All I was doing was teaching my kids to understand the importance of working hard, but also working smart. I wanted them to know their worth and embrace the limitless possibilities that lie ahead. Just because they are teenagers does not mean they have to settle for the typical teen wage. Who said they couldn't make $40 an hour? Lawn mowing doesn't require decades of labor-force experience, after all.

My goal was to instill in my children the belief that there are no limits to their income potential. They have the power to shape their own reality and seize every opportunity that comes their way. Plus, I wanted them to understand the beauty of time freedom: setting their own schedules and working hours. No more punching a clock for someone else! And if they wanted to make even more money, they simply had to rinse and repeat the process with more neighbors.

By capitalizing on this real-life opportunity, I hoped to open their eyes to the endless possibilities of wealth creation.

SECTION II
Creating Wealth

CHAPTER 3

Budgeting Is Dead —The Secret of Value-Based Spending

The most precious things in life are not those you get for money.
—ALBERT EINSTEIN

When it comes to creating wealth, the concept of value-based spending is crucial and revolves around three main concepts: fixing money leaks, creating a value-based spending plan (aka the Happiness Formula), and applying millionaire spending habits. Contrary to popular belief, you don't just magically develop better spending habits once you get wealthy. Instead, most wealthy people develop them before. It's those good habits that make them wealthy in the first place.

Value-based spending is the concept that your money should go to things you appreciate and won't take for granted. Some things, like bills, need to be paid—but value-based spending focuses on discretionary income instead of your money situation as a whole.

Regardless of what your spending habits are like right now, this chapter will give you actionable advice that you can use to create generational wealth. I want to help you align your spending habits with your values, which will make it easier for you to achieve the goals you've put in place. I'm beyond excited to teach you this, so let's dive into the first concept of value-based spending: fixing money leaks (and no, not through a budget).

Budgeting Is Dead

B-u-d-g-e-t. Six terrifying letters. When people hear the word "budget," they often think of financial austerity or self-deprivation. Other people only think of budgeting when they're trying to save money.

In other cases, people feel like budgeting only makes sense if you *have* money. They don't see the point of it if your income can't cover your expenses or you don't have any money to save.

But let's be honest: Some people take budgeting too seriously. I did too, at first. Sitting down to look at my financial situation like that often gave me a little anxiety. There's something deeply personal about dissecting what you've spent money on for the month that evokes some intense emotions—and I didn't like those feelings one bit. Adding a partner to the mix only amplifies the anxiety.

If any of those situations sound familiar to you, you're not alone. Most people don't like doing an overview of their financial situation every month. But that's also why *most people don't create generational wealth.*

Don't worry—this chapter isn't going to be a budgeting exercise. Instead, we're going to turn the concept of budgeting on its head. From here on out, budgeting is *dead.*

Going forward, we won't be calling the tracking of your income and expenses a "budget." No, the new term is your "personal balance sheet." The goal of this exercise is to help you "find money" by plugging your money leaks and redirecting those funds into supporting your life values and long-term goals.

Ready to get started? Get out a pen and paper, or open up a spreadsheet on your computer, and follow along.

Step 1: Tracking Your Income

The first step to creating your balance sheet is tracking your income. Now, as simple as this part sounds, a lot of people don't do it correctly. When they hear "track your income," they only focus on the money they make from one or two sources. That's not the case here.

I want you to write down *all* the money that you make throughout the month, from every single source. So that's the money you make from your job, your interest and dividend payments, your side hustle, your business, your real estate holdings, and any other investment you may have.

It's important to have a clear picture of your income so you know accurately where your money is going.

Step 2: Track Your Expenses

Once you've got all your income categorized and in one place, it's time to move on to the second step in creating your balance sheet: tracking your expenses. You need at least three months of data to help you make some important decisions. In this area, you want both larger-ticket expenses like taxes, housing payments (PITI), loan payments (school, bank, car, etc.), credit card payments, and insurance (health, life, etc.), as well as smaller-ticket ones—groceries, utilities, shopping, gifts, travel, and household expenses.

Even though you're tracking everything, the larger-ticket expenses are where you want to make the most changes. Sure, saving $100 on your grocery bill each month would be good, but slicing $1,000 off loan payments each month would be even better. The big-ticket expenses will move the needle and actually propel you to financial independence. We will cover this more in-depth in Section 3.

Step 3: Get Leverage

Once you've got everything written down, it's time to move on to using a tool that will help you keep track of your personal balance sheet from month to month. Keeping it on a piece of paper or in a spreadsheet isn't a bad idea, but we want something that will be much easier to use and that you can keep up with every single day.

My personal recommendation for a tool in this category is Empower. com (formerly known as PersonalCapital.com). Empower.com is an account aggregator platform with bank-level security. In addition to helping you identify your income and expenses, Empower.com helps you to automatically track your assets and liabilities, has a portfolio fee analyzer, and can even generate projections based on your balance sheets. It's truly a powerful tool that can greatly help you along your wealth journey.

I've used it for my own balance sheet over the years, and it helped me figure out where my money was going—the first step to plugging money leaks.

However, if you're not a fan of Empower.com, other options exist, like Simplifi.com or You Need a Budget (YNAB.com). However, they are not as robust as Empower.com when it comes to analyzing and projecting portfolio performance, which will be important as we progress. Though Simplifi.com and YNAB do have *some* portfolio analyzer features, they don't automatically generate the granular results you need; you'd have to do some of that analysis yourself.

The whole goal of this exercise is to make plugging your money leaks and organizing your balance sheet as simple and easy as possible. Complexity is the enemy of execution.

All that I've mentioned earlier is useless if you don't actually take the time to apply it. You *need* to take massive action right now if you want this to work. So, put a bookmark right here and do these three things.

1. Open an Empower.com account
2. Link your bank, credit card, and retirement accounts, so it can aggregate your data all in one place
3. Begin tracking your income and expenses

Step 4: Uncover Where Your Money Is *Really* Going

One thing I like to tell my clients is to think of your financial situation as a boat; whatever kind you want it to be, that's up to you. It's a vessel that's meant to help take you to shore, the goal we discussed in Chapter 2.

However, your negative financial choices are like little holes or leaks in that boat. As tiny as they may be, over time they'll let water in, which will sink your boat—and even if it doesn't sink, it will be a messy ride as you scramble to plug those leaks. The good thing is that most money leaks are reversible. If you find them quickly enough, you can plug them and have a smooth ride to shore.

I like to plug these money leaks with a simple three-step process.

1. Track your expenses to see where you are
2. Categorize where you're spending your money
3. Execute a targeted plan to fix the problems you find in Step 2

In order to do this, you'll need to gather three to six months of data for your expenses using an account aggregation tool like Empower.com (discussed in Step 3). Once you've done that, it's time to sort through your expenses with a fine-tooth comb. When you do, you'll discover that there are four categories of expenses.

- **Destructive Expenses:** These are the worst kinds of expenses to have. They push you toward debt and poverty—things like drugs, overspending on alcohol, excessive credit card bills, and paying exorbitant fees that could be avoided with proper planning. For example, one of my clients would buy purses and shoes every time she felt stressed. Needless to say, she had a LOT of purses and shoes!
- **Consumptive Expenses:** These types of expenses aren't as bad as destructive expenses, but don't help you in the long run. They don't build income or assets and should be appropriately managed so

they don't become destructive. Think of them as lifestyle expenses. I remember discussing this with my husband—he splurged for Sirius Radio over the holidays. It costs around $30 per month per vehicle, but he only listens to *one* radio channel in one car.

- **Protective Expenses:** These expenses help us keep our wealth— things like accounting fees, tax preparation, health and property insurance, and legal fees. Planned spending on these items will help you keep more of your money in the long run.
- **Productive Expenses:** These are the "best" kinds of expenses to have on your balance sheet. They enhance your life right now and will also help you in the future. I like to think of it this way: If you spend a dollar on a productive expense, you're going to get more than a dollar from it in the future. Some of my favorite examples of this are investing $40 in a deal analysis app that helps you underwrite property faster and make better deals, or hiring a virtual assistant to take on your administrative work so you can concentrate on finding your next investment.

I want you to go through your expenses for the past three to six months and itemize everything, putting them in one of the four categories listed above. To make it easier for you, I've put together a list of expenses that fall into each category below.

Expense Key

DESTRUCTIVE EXPENSES

- Addictive habits
- Drug use
- Excessive dining out
- Overdraft fees
- Credit card debt
- Monthly memberships not being used, e.g., gym memberships, online memberships
- Mortgage payments over 50% income
- Anything to excess, e.g., spoiling kids with too many gifts, compulsive shopping, television use to excess
- Gambling
- Overleverage of bank money in real estate
- Overleverage of credit score
- Overfinancing of cars
- Investing ALL home equity without reserve account

Destructive expenses push you toward debt/poverty.

CONSUMPTIVE EXPENSES

- Paying overage charges on cell phone bill
- Cable or satellite TV
- High-speed internet
- Buying computer games to excess
- Movies, video game rentals
- Pizza every weekend
- Buying new car instead of slightly used
- Mortgage payments between 30% and 50% of income
- Shopping for best price vs. best value
- Not being wise with purchases
- Buying name-brand clothes when you can't afford them
- Shopping at mall instead of discount stores
- Excessive gift purchasing for b-days, Christmas, etc.
- Magazine subscriptions you don't use
- Parties and associated costs
- Eating out
- Vacations
- Spa treatments (could be productive)

Consumptive expenses do not build income or assets, so keep these expenses in check

PROTECTIVE EXPENSES

- Liquid savings (six months of expenses)
- Life insurance
- Disability insurance
- Medical insurance
- Auto insurance
- Emergency preparedness

Protective Expenses, when managed properly, help you keep your wealth.

PRODUCTIVE EXPENSES

- Food
- Clothing
- Housing
- Charitable contribution
- Investing in your education
- Insurance, e.g., life, disability, health, car, home
- Mortgage payments less than 30% of income
- Business expenses for work
- Music lessons
- Setting up a will & trust, e.g., attorney's fees
- Utility payments, e.g., gas, electricity, water, sewer
- Car loan (not upside down)
- Gasoline
- Cell phone bill for business
- Internet service
- Medicines, medical bills
- Savings
- Investing for cash flow and/or future life events

Productive expenses enhance life NOW and in the FUTURE. $1 spent now potentially gives you $1+ in the future.

This exercise will give you a good idea of where most of your money is going. Once you've identified that, it's time to start plugging your money leaks. After all, knowledge without application won't bring us any of the results we're after.

Step 5: Taking Action—Plugging Your Money Leaks

At the beginning of this chapter, I said budgeting is dead and you should spend according to your values. And all of your hard work up until now has been laying the groundwork to take massive action: understanding where you are currently spending, plugging those money leaks, and freeing up cash to put toward your goals, dreams, and, dare I say, values you actually want! So let's get to it!

Eliminate ANY Destructive Expenses

If anything falls into the destructive category, we eliminate it *immediately*. So, getting rid of excessive eating out, any addictive habits you may have, cutting out drug use, overindulgence in alcohol, overdraft fees, and credit card debt—all of that has to go. Now, I know it's easier said than done, but this part is nonnegotiable if you want to create a wealthy life for yourself. You're not weak if you can't do it alone. In fact, I recommend seeking counseling or other holistic services if you need help to take the big leap.

Reduce Your Consumptive Expenses

For the expenses that fall into the consumptive category, we want to reduce those as much as we can. This includes things like taking on a new car payment when your old car that's paid off works just fine, eating out, traveling, paying for similar or duplicate services, and even subscriptions that you don't use often enough to justify their cost. Focus on low-hanging fruit that is easy to reduce or eliminate and can help bolster your savings rate with just a few clicks and a couple of phone calls. No, I'm not saying you need to cut your lifestyle down, but there are always things that you can get rid of in this category that will save you money and won't really impact your life.

This is actually an exercise my husband and I do every year—we make all our expenses "re-interview" to be in our expense plan. It is very simple really. In November, we simply review our current annual expenses during our annual goal-setting meeting and label them again (destructive, consumptive, protective, or productive). This process goes fairly quickly since we have been tracking all year long with a tool like

Empower.com. Even for pros like us, we always find sneaky subscriptions that we are no longer using and ways to reduce our consumptive expenses, and we take the opportunity to renegotiate our protective and productive expenses. It helps keep us on track financially!

Negotiate/Renegotiate Your Protective Expenses

After you've done both of those things, it's time to look at your protective expenses. We want these expenses, but it doesn't mean that we can't look at them under a microscope. Review and renegotiate these expenses annually to ensure you're getting the best deals to suit your needs. You should be ruthless and honest about what you need for these expenses and consider if your needs have changed from the previous year. For things like insurance and legal and accounting fees, you can negotiate on an annual basis.

It's also important to ensure you're not suckered into paying more than you should for high-priced subscription plans. You could be overpaying for car insurance just because you've been with the same "friend" for years, especially when there are comparable policies out there. Shop around a little and see where you can cut costs.

Monitor Your Productive Expenses

Last, though productive expenses are the best kind of expenses to have, you want to watch these like a hawk—especially in your creating, keeping, and growing wealth phases. You need to be honest with yourself when you overspend in this area, even though these expenses can enhance your life now and in the future. Your productive expenses should be proportionate to your income—as you grow your income from assets, *then* you can expand your spending. Not before.

I see many real estate investors pay thousands of dollars annually for tax planning services, when finding an accountant who will do strategy planning by the hour will most likely work just fine when you just have a few properties under your belt. Some end up overpaying for big legal structures when they don't even own any investments yet!

With this guide in hand, I want to use the chart from a few pages earlier to create your plan to plug the money leaks in your boat that fall into one of these four categories. This exercise is key to creating wealth, and I'm positive you'll come away feeling even more motivated on your journey.

The Happiness Formula: Unlocking Your Spending Values

Now that we've gone through the Budgeting Is Dead process and taken action with your expenses, let's talk about phase two: the Happiness Formula (i.e., unlocking your spending values).

I'm sure you've picked up by now that I am a huge proponent of changing the way you think before you can change your life. It's a principle I've found in every single success story. Regardless of what you're trying to achieve, changing your mindset will help you change your life.

Let me introduce you to the Happiness Formula. Yes, it sounds a little woo-woo, but I promise that it's not about *wishing* for things to change. Instead, this exercise is rooted in action. We're going to find out what it is that truly makes you happy.

This exercise is interactive. Read it through first, and then once more while following the steps. If you don't do it, you won't get results. This part of this book is dedicated to helping you create wealth, and this formula is a key part of creating the mindset that will lead you to make your financial goals a reality.

Right off the bat, you might be a little unsure of what exactly makes you happy. Don't worry about that!

I like to start off this exercise by helping my clients figure out what *doesn't* make them happy. We all have a good idea of what isn't working for us, what makes us miserable, or at the very least uncomfortable with how things are currently unfolding.

Step 1: Name What Doesn't Make You Happy

On a blank sheet of paper, take a few minutes to write down all the commitments in your life. You should include *everything* that doesn't make you happy, like people who suck the oxygen out of you, and meetings or scheduled commitments on your calendar that you're not excited about. Don't worry if you feel a bit of discomfort writing these things down. It's fine. I'm not asking you to act. Right now, we just want to identify everything in your life that's causing you discomfort.

Next on that sheet, I want you to write down any investment you've gotten yourself into that's been weighing on your mind. It can be a real estate investment, a stock you've bought, a start-up that you've invested in, a business deal, or even a work deal that you've committed to. Whatever the case, it is something that stresses you out, something you want to get out from underneath, or something you wish you hadn't invested in in the first place.

Last, I want you to write down all the stuff you've accumulated over the years that doesn't make you happy, takes up unnecessary space in your home, or you can live without. Believe it or not, I'm in the process of getting rid of things in my own home right now. I do this every single quarter, and *every time without fail*, there's something to get rid of.

When you've got all these things written down, sit with it for a while. Again, don't be worried about acting on anything you have on your paper. This exercise is all about acknowledging what isn't making you happy, so you can take the next step and focus on what would make you happy. Once you've done that, it's time to move on to the next step.

Step 2: Identifying Your Happiness Formula

Here, we're going to look at what truly makes you happy—the first step in coming up with your personal Happiness Formula that will keep you motivated and help you create the life you dream of.

I attended a conference once where Vishen Lakhiani said that true happiness is found at the intersection of three things: our experiences, our growth, and our contributions.[6] I've found this to be true in my life, which is why the next few questions are all about figuring out those three things in your own life.

What do you want to experience?

Get out another sheet of paper. First, I want you to ask yourself what kind of experiences you want to have in life. What do you want to do or experience in your city or town? What do you want to do or experience in your country? What international experiences do you want to have? Give this some real thought and write down what makes you feel good when you think about it.

If you're in a relationship, you should have your partner do this as well, and even your children. It's a great way for the whole family to work on their mindset. When my family did this, our goals looked like visiting more local restaurants, going to music and cultural events with my husband, and visiting the national parks to help our daughter collect her Junior Ranger badges, with the occasional "big trip" adventure sprinkled in.

---

6   Vishen Lakhiani and Irina Yugay, "The Problem with Goal Setting and What You Can Do Instead: The 3 Most Important Questions," *Mindvalley* (blog), May 20, 2022, https://blog.mindvalley.com/3miqs/.

How do you want to grow?

The next thing I want you to write down on that paper relates to growth. In what ways do you want to improve your mindset? Your skills? Your network? Think this through and ask yourself: What kind of person do you need to be to make your goals a reality? What kind of classes do you need to take? What kind of books do you need to read? What kind of skills do you need to pick up?

This section doesn't only have to be about work—it can also entail personal aspirations that you have to improve the quality of your life. We humans thrive on growth, progress, and momentum.

When I did this part of the exercise, I knew immediately some of the growth I needed to do professionally involved public speaking and networking. Personally, I wanted to become a better cook and gardener as well, and I needed help with those too.

How do you want to give back?

The last thing you're going to write down is about contribution, namely the ways that you want to contribute to your family and, by extension, society. You can contribute in three ways: time, money, and knowledge. Contributing in these three ways can look different for each person, and it's all dependent on what you want your life to look like.

- **Time:** You can contribute time outside your household through activities like volunteering, but also inside as well! Often you don't realize that what you're doing inside your household (raising empathetic, resilient, intelligent children, for example) can have a great impact on the world. That's a valuable contribution of time.
- **Money:** You can choose how you want to contribute money. Is it by donating to charities or nonprofit organizations focused on causes you support? Or do you prefer to help people yourself, on a more personal basis? How you do it is entirely up to you and depends on what makes you feel the best.
- **Knowledge:** This is one of my favorite ways to contribute. Regardless of how you feel about yourself, so many people could benefit from learning from you, even about the things you take for granted. How do you want to share your knowledge with others? You can think of contributing through local community classes, or even free online classes like I do at AshWealth.com.

It's totally fine to spend some time figuring all of this out. Again, I don't expect you to complete this part of the exercise on your first pass.

I want you to spend some time thinking about it, so you can write down what you *actually* want.

In fact, this Happiness Formula is something that I do on a regular basis—at first quarterly, then biannually—to ensure that I'm actually aligned with what I want and not just moving through life mindlessly. It also helps to revisit this list because you're going to check things off as you accomplish them.

Step 3: Setting the Scene to Make Changes

Setting up your life for success is probably the most important part of the Happiness Formula. This might be the most difficult part, but it's *so* worth it when you start to see results in your life. Just like the steps before, I want you to get out a piece of paper and follow along as we peel back the layers on what will truly make you happy.

What do you need to change in your environment?

First, I want you to look at your environment in four important areas: your health, your mental state, your home life, and your work life. It's important this is an *honest* look, as this step is all about making changes to improve your life. Ask yourself questions like:

- Are there any health changes I need to make?
- Are there any actions I need to take that will improve my mental health?
- What do I need to do to improve my home life?
- What is required to make my work life more enjoyable?

Heavy questions, I know. But the answers you'll find after examining your responses to these questions *honestly* will change your life and make you truly happy. Taking control of your life can be scary at first, but the results are always satisfying.

Who do you need in your life?

Next, it's time to take stock of the people in your life. This one can be difficult for many reasons, as it's often hard to pull back from people who may be negatively affecting us—especially if they are lifelong friends or family members.

However, we aren't doing this exercise to get rid of people as much as we are to understand who you need to add to your life. Are there any peers and mentors you would like to add to your circle that will make your life easier and help you achieve your goals faster? If yes, write down their names. And if you don't have names, write down the kind of expertise you want them to have.

I particularly love this part of the Happiness Formula, as it really helps you to see opportunities you might have overlooked in the past.

What kind of support do you need on your journey?
Last, I want you to examine your network. There are three things I want you to think about when you consider it.

- Who can you plug into for support on your journey?
- What kind of leverage do you have, and how will you use it?
- Who will you need to hire (a virtual assistant, for example) to help you?

Chances are your network is already very valuable—you just aren't using it to its full potential. This part of the exercise is meant to help you open your eyes to what you have available to you, in hopes that it will start giving you ideas for what you can achieve.

Pulling It All Together: Value-Based Spending

In order to create your own Happiness Formula, you need to be bold about what it is you want and relentless about getting there. To close up this exercise, I am going to leave you with three steps to take all that you've just written down and turn them into an action plan for being boldly happy.

1. Purge the things that weigh you down and give yourself space to thrive
2. Dream about your ideal world—the experiences, the growth, and the contribution
3. Figure out the kind of environment and support that you need to make it a reality

The Happiness Formula isn't static. It constantly changes as you change, which is why I encourage revisiting it often. I like to call it "rinse, improve, and repeat." You already have all that you need to make your ideal world your reality; you just need to organize your life to make it happen—and the Happiness Formula is the best way to help you do that.

Once you've completed the Budgeting Is Dead exercise, you'll realize that you have some extra money that used to be spent on destructive or consumptive expenses. By taking that money and starting your investment journey, you'll grow your assets and wealth with the Happiness Formula as your guide to increase your happiness. As a result, your spending will align more and more with what you value most in life—your financial goals and your happiness!

═══ YOUR CHAPTER ACTION PLAN ═══

1. Complete your Budgeting Is Dead plan.
   - Use software to track all of your income and expenses
   - Categorize your expenses
   - Take action on your expenses to free up money
     - Eliminate destructive expenses
     - Reduce consumptive expenses
     - Renegotiate protective expenses
     - Monitor productive expenses
2. Complete your Happiness Formula exercise.
   - Identify what is not making you happy
   - Identify what would make you happy (experiences, growth, contribution)
   - Set up your environment for success

Real Stories of Money for Tomorrow
PRINCIPLES IN ACTION

Investing as a Couple—Liz Faircloth, cofounder,
The Real Estate InvestHER and DeRosa Capital, and
Matt Faircloth, cofounder, DeRosa Capital

"If we don't change something, we are headed for divorce."

Those were the exact words that Matt shared with me during one of the toughest moments of our seventeen years of being married. Let me bring you back to that time in our lives. It was 2008. I had just quit my job to join Matt full-time in our real estate investing business. Around the same time I quit my job, the market crashed, and we had made some tough investment decisions that included buying a vacant 10,000-square-foot building.

Moreover, we were making a ton of mistakes when working and investing together. Not only were the outside conditions stressful, but how we were treating each other was piling on additional stress, both emotionally and financially.

It's easy to see now, but here are the mistakes we were making as a couple.

1. Not investing in all of the important entities: marriage, business, and each other
2. Lack of clarity and ownership of roles and responsibilities
3. Poor communication and lack of communication in both our work and personal lives

Thankfully, over the course of the next several years, we stayed committed to growing our wealth, growing our relationship, and growing ourselves. It was not easy, but we were committed to building a bigger life together. To grow a bigger life together, you need to grow on many different levels.

During the next several years, we shifted our relationship from being on "rocky grounds" to thriving together, 10x-ing our multifamily portfolio (both by geography and size of projects), and doubling our wealth.

Here are the three areas we focused on improving in order to thrive together.

1. Focusing on one another's needs, the marriage's needs, and the business's needs
2. Clarity and ownership of roles and responsibilities
3. Exceptional and continual communication

Let me show you how to put these three principles into action!

Focusing on one another, the marriage, and the business

It is really easy to make your investing business the primary focus, or if you have kids, they become the most important focus. However, you need to make your marriage your primary focus. *Never forget this.* It's never last; it is always first. You need to make weekly and monthly time for cultivating your relationship with date nights and enjoying one another's company. Remember, you schedule what you value.

Next, your business needs attention and focus. You need to schedule monthly meetings to discuss your investing goals, what is working (and not working), and your finances. So many couples we know have these discussions while making dinner or getting the kids ready in the morning. Stop talking about business while eating dinner or doing some other task. Keep these business discussions for focused meeting time.

During one of our regular business meetings coming out of the 2008 market crash, we discussed where we needed to focus. We decided to do more of what was working for us—raising capital and buying multifamily. As soon as we decided to focus on these two things, our business and investments grew significantly. As the old saying goes, what you focus on expands.

Next, each person in the relationship needs attention and focus. I have supported Matt to take care of his health, attend masterminds, and grow himself spiritually. Matt has supported me with my own journey, mastermind weekends, and training for races. Never lose sight that in every relationship there are two people who need individual attention and support.

Gaining clarity and ownership of roles and responsibilities

Regardless of whether one partner is the "active" person running the investments and the other person is more "supportive," or you have two people who are both active in the business working together, getting clarity on roles, along with 100 percent ownership of these roles, is critical. In order to gain this clarity of roles and responsibilities, we are big fans of doing a deep dive into our personalities, skills, interests, and experiences. Once you are clear on one another's roles, ensure you are clear on what it means to "own" this role as well.

Cultivating exceptional and consistent communication

The number-one reason couples are not growing together in life, in business, or in their wealth is the lack of communication. Our first recommendation is to identify whether you and your partner are over-communicators or under-communicators. There is no right or wrong communication style; rather, you must identify where you are and ensure you are adapting to meet the needs of your partner.

The second recommendation to grow in communication is to have a weekly conversation about your relationship. We suggest a simple yet profound exercise called "Continue, Start, Stop, and Do." Here is the question you want to answer on your own and then share with your partner: What do I want/need (my partner) to Continue, Start, Stop, and Do to deepen our relationship? This is not always easy to answer, but the answers to these questions are incredibly helpful so each partner can make adjustments along the way and know how to meet each other's needs.

Wrapping Up

Just like anything that is outstanding in your life, growing and keeping wealth as a couple takes energy, focus, and time. It is hard to grow wealth if you are not communicating well, adjusting to one another's needs, and growing as a couple and individually.

We are passionate about helping couples do this, so look for a book from us to be released soon!

CHAPTER 4

The Wealth Formula —Two Principles the 1 Percent Master to Create Wealth

Results are simple: learn, plan, do, repeat.
Most people fail at the last two steps.

Since we've covered your mindset and talked about how to build the foundation for wealth, it's time to get started with the fun part—actually *creating* wealth.

For the rest of this book, when I mention wealth, I'm talking about your *why* (I helped you to discover it in Chapter 2). Now we're going to dive into the formula for creating wealth.

The wealth formula is simple and is predicated on two basic concepts. First, you move from linear income, or trading your time for dollars, to residual income, which is investing in assets that produce income regardless of your involvement. Second, you create a "wealthy balance sheet"—this is when your assets cover your expenses, and then some.

I know you're excited about this part. I am too! This section on wealth creation is one of my favorite parts to teach my coaching clients. There's something about watching them discover what's possible for the first time—seeing the light bulbs go off above their heads, witnessing them experience that first real spark when they *know* that what they want to achieve is going to happen—that's completely indescribable. I'm preparing you to have that light bulb moment too.

Shifting Your Income from Linear to Residual

If you're thinking that the idea of linear versus residual income sounds familiar, you'd be correct. Learning to shift your income from trading time for dollars (linear) to owning assets that cover all of your expenses (residual) is a required move on the path to financial freedom. It has been covered extensively in books like *Rich Dad's Cashflow Quadrant*, *MONEY: Master the Game*, and *The Automatic Millionaire*, as well as many others. I'll sum it up in the chart below.

Linear Income vs Residual Passive Income

Active Income Trading Time for Money	Passive Income Not Dependent on Your Presence
EMPLOYEE *You have a job* **TIME = $** No leverage	**BUSINESS OWNER** *You own a system and* *people work for you* **PEOPLE = $$$** Leverage
SELF-EMPLOYED *You own a job* **TIME = $$** No leverage	**INVESTOR** *Money works for you* **$$$ = $$$$$$** Passive income

On the left side of the chart, we see people who are active income earners, or what I like to call *linear earners*. Notice that employees and the self-employed occupy this side of the chart. Both situations involve trading time for money.

The employee gets a paycheck each week or month directly tied to the number of hours they spent at their job during that pay period.

The self-employed, on the other hand, own a job, but they often must work in the business to get paid, even though they might be their own boss—think lawyers, doctors, chiropractors, engineers, and consultants.

Compared to employees, the self-employed are often paid much more for their work since they don't have a boss taking a cut of their earnings, but there's still little leverage.

In both of these situations, if you don't work, you don't earn anything, which makes it next to impossible to create lasting wealth. You might be able to create some wealth, but not at the level you want to accomplish your dreams. Think back to your *why*. In order to have the freedom to make your *why* a reality, you need leverage.

Both situations on the left side of the graph pay the highest amount of taxes. Why? The tax code in the United States and many other countries around the world incentivizes business owners and investors. Business owners and investors drive the economy. On the other hand, very few tax breaks are given to employees and the self-employed.

The goal is to move from the left to the right side of the chart as quickly as possible, to create wealth for yourself and your family. On the right side of the chart, income becomes passive, or *residual,* as I like to call it—what you earn isn't dependent on you being physically present. The two types of people on this side of the chart are business owners and investors.

Maintaining a Business Doesn't Make You a Business Owner

There's a common fallacy about business ownership: A lot of people believe that once they own a business, they're automatically a business owner. That's surprisingly not the case. You only truly move from self-employed to business owner if **the business can run largely without you for a year or two.** To achieve this, you would need a proven system, as well as employees who can handle everything with very little of your guidance or input. That's what the real goal of business ownership should be.

The threshold of getting to that point where your business largely runs without you varies—depending on your business, you could have five employees or fifty employees. In today's digital landscape and depending on your industry, you can achieve critical mass with a lot fewer employees. Maybe you'd still have to spend a few minutes each week on your business and attend a few board meetings per year, but you would have a lot of leverage (other people's time, knowledge, and expertise) and start to regain your freedom.

Even for business owners, investing should become the end goal. It's the pinnacle of residual income—when your money starts to work for you. Investors don't own a business; they invest in someone else's business and reap the rewards of others' time, knowledge, expertise, and hard work. This is where true leverage comes in: You're truly able to step away and live the life of your dreams.

The True Freedom of Leverage

Most of the time, the value of leverage is recognized when everything in your life goes wrong. A case in point happened to my family in 2018.

My husband had been severely injured mountain biking. At the time, we didn't know how badly he had been hurt; even though he took an eight-foot fall right onto his head, he was discharged from the hospital that day with only some pain meds. But by that night, his situation took a turn for the worse.

My husband couldn't stand on his own. His eyes were unequally dilated, and he kept falling over. We took him to another hospital, which diagnosed him with a major concussion and two broken vertebrae in his neck. He had to wear a cervical collar for several months and needed to undergo grueling rehabilitation.

With several houses in the middle of rehab, no help running investments, and a solo mentoring practice, I didn't have time or attention to spare. All of this was on top of my full-time job and the caretaker responsibilities of a small child and my two grandparents. I had to pick up the phone and call my property manager to let them know that I needed at least two to three weeks off to take care of my husband. I was working *in* my business and not *on* it, which left me with so much to do.

And then three weeks later, my mom passed away at home. My whole world came crashing down around me. Instead of being away from my business for weeks, I needed to step away for months. This experience really put everything into perspective for me.

Money was coming into my bank account in droves. My mentoring business was launching. I thought I had tremendous momentum. But in reality, I was stuck on the self-employment quadrant on the left side, when I needed to be on the right side. I needed to make a change. I needed to step away and continue earning an income. I owed that to myself and my family.

Although building your own business can be very financially rewarding, most people are not cut out for that type of hard work, dedication, and uncertainty. Even if you own your own business, investing in other people's businesses is a great way to create diversification and passive wealth.

I want you to spend some time thinking about your current situation. Which side of the chart are you on? If you had to step away from your life tomorrow, how long would you be able to go without your income stream drying up? Are you satisfied with that length of time? Does it feel like enough?

That dissatisfaction you feel is good—it's part of the fuel you'll need to start making the changes now that will help you create wealth and lead to generational wealth for your family. Let's consider the next part of the Wealth Formula: the wealthy balance sheet.

Balance Sheets: Poor, Middle-Class, and Wealthy

Learning how to create a wealthy balance sheet is another foundational move for your path to financial freedom and is covered extensively in other financial books. Conceptually, a wealthy balance sheet is simply one in which your assets bring in enough passive income to cover all of your expenses. However, most Americans fall short and have a poor or middle-class balance sheet instead—one that keeps them from experiencing true wealth.

The "Poor" Balance Sheet

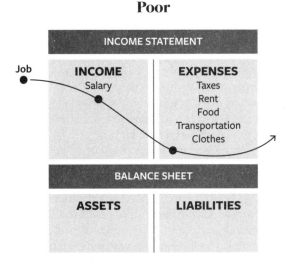

Poor

Someone with a "poor" balance sheet is generally an employee (on the left side of the chart from the previous section). Their income is an hourly wage or possibly a set salary that may or may not be enough to cover all their expenses. Moreover, they may have more than one job just to make ends meet. They do not have assets or liabilities simply because they can't afford to get into debt. Furthermore, they have no disposable income to set aside in savings for emergencies, let alone for investing in assets. More times than not, someone with a "poor" balance sheet is living paycheck to paycheck and is likely not in a position to get ahead in life.

The Middle-Class Balance Sheet

Middle Class

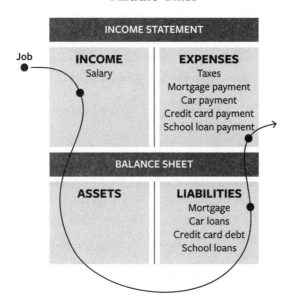

The middle-class balance sheet has a few extra steps, but the same end result—their salary goes first to pay for their liabilities like a mortgage, car loans, student loans, and credit cards, then their living expenses. They don't have any assets that are working for them, and would still be on the left side of the previous chart, but possibly in the self-employed group instead of being employees. This is the typical American dream that so many people aspire to. Why?

When you're in the middle class, you hold on to the idea that somehow you'll get out of the rat race, maybe by saving money in a bank account or investing in a retirement account. But stocks, bonds, and mutual funds have failed many people. That strategy relies on accumulating a huge amount of money to *maybe* withdraw 3 to 4 percent per year when you hit retirement age. Additionally, you need your portfolio to grow every single year so you don't end up losing money.

Yes, technically you can call a 401(k) an asset, but it doesn't kick off income that you can use *right now*. So, how do we overcome this? What are the truly wealthy doing?

The Wealthy Balance Sheet

Wealthy

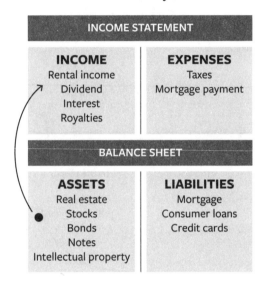

The wealthy take their active income—earned from a salary, savings, businesses they own, or even an inheritance—and use that money to buy assets. Maybe they start with stocks, bonds, and mutual funds with a higher yield, but they move on to real estate, notes, other property (e.g., passive real estate, private equity, hedge funds), and even building/ scaling their own businesses. The money generated from those assets is what they use to cover their expenses and their liabilities.

Another thing you'll notice on the balance sheet of the wealthy: They don't have many consumer liabilities. Most of their liabilities will be in the form of a mortgage on a rental property or something similar. Their debt comes from purchasing an asset that will provide an income stream greater than the cost of the debt, thus making them money in the long run. We're working toward this end goal.

What Counts as an Asset?

You probably have a good idea of what counts as an asset, but let's look at it through the lens of wealth creation.

Assets are things that put money in your pocket in the future, like:

- Savings (as long as it's earning more than inflation!)
- Stocks
- Mutual funds
- Certificates of deposit
- Real estate
- Businesses/intellectual property
- Precious metals

On the other hand, liabilities are things that take money out of your pocket. You spend money on these every month—and they still count as liabilities even if you are spending money in support of an asset, like a mortgage on your primary residence or other real estate you own. Assets and liabilities are not mutually exclusive. Sometimes, assets will have a liability attached to them. Other common liabilities are:

- Loan balances (school, car, bank, etc.)
- Credit card debt
- Business loan balances

However, when we're talking about assets and liabilities, I'm sure you can pinpoint things that you have spent money on or received as a gift that you hope will increase in value in the future. I'm talking about things like:

- Car collection
- Gun or knife collection
- Vinyl record collection
- Stamp collection
- Grandma's china
- Jewelry collection
- Art collection
- Baseball card collection

You might be acquiring these in hopes of being able to sell them at an increased value at some time in the future. Things like these are *not* assets. Until you sell them for a profit, they are actually liabilities or expenses, and should be classified as such when you do this exercise. It might be a hard truth to swallow, but you should avoid lying to yourself about this. Having a clear understanding of what constitutes an asset versus a liability is important to setting the foundation that we'll use to help you build generational wealth.

Here are a few examples of things that my family members thought were assets that I've had to dispose of during estate settlements. While these "assets" hold quite a bit of sentimental value, they arguably don't hold any real financial value, let alone generate a monthly income to get anyone to financial freedom.

- My mom's three sets of china and Americana crystal
- My dad's gun and knife collections
- My grandfather's coin collection and OU football memorabilia

The Balance Sheet Journey

The truth is most of us start off with our income statement looking like the "poor" one. I started there too. When you're self-made, *you start poor.* You get your first job out of college and your income grows over the years. But with smart use of your money, plus consistent and persistent action toward a sound investing plan, your balance sheet can look more like the "wealthy" balance sheet. This allows your children (or other heirs) to start off on the wealthy side with the trust fund you leave for them. Or if you decide to not leave them a trust fund, you leave them a proven road map and the education they can use to create their own wealthy balance sheet (more about this in Section IV).

The Tale of Two Grandfathers

To illustrate my point, I want to tell you the story of my two grandfathers: my mother's father, Grandfather #1; and my father's father, Grandfather #2. Both of my grandfathers had similar circumstances. So much so that you could say they had largely the same opportunities.

Both of them were in the Army Air Corps (basically the Air Force before it became the Air Force), and both were honorably discharged after World War II and turned to homesteading and hunting to keep their expenses low. They both raised their own cattle for personal use and for sale, so they had extra income coming in. Both of my grandfathers had full-time jobs in the oil industry as well, and they both had oil on their properties in Oklahoma.

Despite having congruent lives, Grandfather #1 died nearly penniless in a nursing home, but Grandfather #2 lived his final years in an upscale assisted-living facility with his second wife, and was able to pass on a sizable inheritance to his heirs. What caused the drastic change in circumstances?

Their paths diverged when it came time to choose a retirement plan. Grandfather #1 took the more traditional path, the one most middle-class people do once they retire: He sold his land outright to the oil company, including his cattle; bought an RV to travel and fish; and lived off his pension. Not a bad idea on the face of it, but because he chose to cash out and live off a fixed lump sum, the money ran out thanks to health issues and servicing liabilities.

Grandfather #2 took a different approach. He kept his land and his cattle—to this day, none of us know exactly how he did it, and unfortunately it's a secret he took to the grave with him. We can speculate, though. He chose to grow his land holdings, buying property from neighbors to grow his mineral rights portfolio and receive royalties from drilling. He also wrote the occasional real estate private note and pocketed the interest as income. At 82, my grandfather bought a computer. I drove to and from my college campus to visit him and teach him how to use it so he could trade stocks and manage his money.

He made all the money he earned from his job and in his later years, cattle and oil and gas royalties worked for him. His strategy wasn't perfect, but he definitely moved from middle class to wealthy because of the choices he made about his retirement.

These two concepts (linear versus residual income and the wealthy balance sheet) are essential to creating wealth, and they make up the Wealth Formula that will help you make your dream life possible.

How can we make sure we keep the wealth that we create? We'll take a look at that in the next chapter.

═══ YOUR CHAPTER ACTION PLAN ═══

1. List your assets.
2. List your liabilities.
3. List how much monthly income your assets bring in for you. Do your assets bring in enough passive income to cover all of your expenses?
4. Identify which of the "balance sheets" yours currently looks like.

Real Stories of Money for Tomorrow
PRINCIPLES IN ACTION

Trish Baker, founder, Remote Host Hub

My real estate journey began in 2014, five years before I took the leap to purchase my first property, during a period filled with anticipation and eagerness. Back then, I worked as an accountant, and my husband was a CPA, both of us engrossed in the demands of our careers while raising our two young children. Real estate had captivated my interest for years, and I had even explored the possibility of owning duplexes. However, at that time, I couldn't envision long-term rentals providing the income I desired, leaving me hesitant and lacking the confidence to make the investment plunge.

Fast-forward to 2019, and my focus shifted to acquiring a short-term rental property (STR)—an investment that promised both increased income and additional benefits. Accounting, as a profession, often meant enduring long hours, stringent billable time, and relentless deadlines. I longed for a change that would grant me the ability to attend all of my children's school functions, travel whenever our hearts desired, and regain control over my work schedule.

Why an STR? Growing up, my family had rented homes in the beautiful Pocono Mountains of Pennsylvania. As an adult, I loved going up to the Poconos to go skiing in the winter, and I also knew that it was a year-round destination with lots of hiking, swimming, and rafting. Thinking STRs might be my real estate investing answer, I explored a few properties, yet none compelled me enough to make an offer. Then, unexpectedly, a few months into my search, I received the upsetting news of being laid off from my job. The partnership I worked for was dissolving, abruptly ending my employment. At that moment, a mix of emotions coursed through me, but surprisingly, disappointment was absent. It was an awakening, a profound realization that this turn of events signaled the need for a change in my life.

With this layoff, I found myself at a crossroads: I could embark on the search for another accounting job, continuing to trade my time for money, or I could seize the opportunity to finally embrace real estate investing. The choice became crystal clear. The corporate world no longer held any appeal for me; my heart wasn't in it anymore. With unwavering determination, I made the pivotal decision to whole-heartedly commit to real estate investing.

I diligently examined every property that met my investment criteria listed on the MLS. I went a step further and considered properties listed directly by the owners, which eventually led me to discover my first STR property. Despite the seller receiving two other offers, I recognized the value of the house and decided it was worthwhile to make an offer above the asking price. With confidence, I submitted my offer, and, fortunately, it was accepted.

And so, in the landscape of the Pocono Mountains, I discovered my first STR property—a single investment that would transform my life in countless ways. After my first property, I had the confidence to keep going and in the next year, I bought two more properties. In a short amount of time, I was able to replace my income on real estate alone. I was working way less and spending more time doing what I loved doing: traveling with my family, volunteering at my children's schools, and going to their sporting events.

Since the acquisition of my first STR, I have continued to build my portfolio in real estate and other passive income streams. Having multiple streams of income holds significant importance from my perspective. I learned this lesson the hard way when I experienced the unexpected reality of being let go from my position. Once I shifted my income from linear to residual by adding multiple streams of residual income, my whole life changed for the better.

I know taking control of your financial future can feel hard and scary, especially when you are trying something new. However, I have come to realize that with determination and continuous learning, success becomes inevitable. Having learned these lessons firsthand, my business partner and I are determined to share our experiences and insights, guiding others toward a life of financial independence and freedom through STR investing. In the end, you don't have to trade time for money. Moreover, betting on oneself and prioritizing self-education is an invaluable asset that can never be taken away.

SECTION III
Keeping Wealth

CHAPTER 5

Millionaire Spending Habits

Too many people spend money they earned to buy things they don't want, to impress people that they don't like.

—WILL ROGERS

Once you start creating wealth, you'll need a plan for keeping it. That's what this chapter is all about—how to create habits and systems that will safeguard the wealth you've created. The good thing about this book is you can start applying what you learn in this chapter *right now* to ensure your current assets are safeguarded, as well as set a solid foundation for the wealth you are going to create.

By retirement you'll want to be at least a millionaire—if that weren't true, you likely wouldn't be reading this book about creating generational wealth. I want to share with you what I've learned on my own journey to becoming a self-made millionaire, as well as what other millionaires have credited as helpful on their path to a seven-figure net worth (and beyond!).

What Does the Everyday Millionaire Look Like?

Popular media has conditioned us to think millionaires spend lavishly on cars, homes, and vacations; they're sipping margaritas on a private beach on a tropical island without a care in the world. I used to think that when I was younger too.

But let me tell you, being a millionaire is *nothing* like that. I can tell you that from experience. I'd challenge you to follow the advice of a millionaire who learned how to *stay* a millionaire. That's who you want to learn from, instead of listening to popular media about millionaires.

Oftentimes, the "everyday" millionaire looks like the average joe next door. They don't drive super fancy cars, spend lavishly on clothes, or take luxurious vacations ... yet!

The everyday millionaire has mastered how to invest their resources wisely and safely. As Gary Keller puts it in the book *The ONE Thing*, success is monotonous, and your everyday millionaire has mastered that monotony and doesn't get distracted by shiny objects, doodads, and keeping up with the Joneses. They didn't inherit their wealth, nor did they scale a massively successful business. The everyday millionaire is someone who became wealthy over time because they mastered the principles outlined in this book and took consistent and persistent action.

But to *become* a millionaire and *stay* a millionaire are two different things altogether.

I've distilled my knowledge about millionaire spending habits into three rules you can start applying in your life *right now* that will help you to make lasting changes and help your financial situation in the long run.

Rule #1: Millionaires Know the Difference between Wants and Needs

I'm not trying to be a smart-ass with this rule, but it is so true. I've found one of the most common habits keeping people from improving their financial situation is getting trapped in the cycle of consumerism disguised as "needs."

But everyday millionaires don't have that problem as often as their non-millionaire counterparts. In fact, everyday millionaires are more likely to look to lower costs on large-ticket items such as cars, houses, and vacations while they're in the process of improving their financial situation. While I'm not saying you need to live in complete and utter abnegation to get ahead, there is a point to be made about what you consider a want versus a need.

Ask yourself some tough questions. Is a brand-new car every three years a need or a want? Is buying new clothes every season a need or a want? Is taking an expensive international vacation every year a need or a want? Which of these choices will allow you to get ahead? When you start to think of your choices honestly, it'll get easier to see where you might be unintentionally sabotaging your own wealth plan.

You might know some millionaires who take expensive vacations, drive luxury vehicles, and wear head-to-toe designer clothes. There are plenty of these people out there. But I'm also sure if you walked up to them and asked when they started splurging on those expensive items, you'd hear the same response nine out of ten times.

It was *after* they achieved significant progress toward their goals.

More importantly, that splurge wasn't made in vain to keep up with the Joneses; rather, it was a calculated splurge to enhance their happiness (think about all those experiences you wrote down during the Happiness Formula exercise).

Avoiding lifestyle creep is one of the biggest ways to secure your path to wealth. Just because your income increases doesn't mean you have to start spending more on cars, houses, clothes, and vacations. By diverting extra income into assets that will generate passive income, you'll create a consistent cash flow, which you can then use to do whatever you like—even splurge.

I have personal experience with this. My husband and I almost bought a new(er) car to replace my 2011 Subaru Outback because we were facing a high repair bill and thought a new(er) car would be better. But in the end, the math won. We took the $50,000-plus we would have spent on a car—a Toyota Tacoma TRD Sport—and invested in a deal that would double our money in five years. We're letting the new investment pay for the new car I'll eventually need.

Being able to take the emotions out of lifestyle decisions and focus on the real-time value of your money is essential to creating wealth!

Rule #2: Millionaires Know How to Create, Save, and Invest Their Income

When you look at the everyday millionaire, their path to wealth often follows the same principles, and it all revolves around making smart moves with their money, like moving from linear to residual income. We'll talk more about what those "smart moves" look like in the next chapter, but for now, we can say that millionaires understand the need to create multiple streams of passive income.

With those multiple income streams, their goal is to move the left side of the cash flow quadrant (employee or self-employed) to the right side (business owner or investor). Over 65 percent of millionaires achieve this through a combination of real estate, business ventures, and stocks.[7]

It's not a linear process. In fact, it's more like a cycle—create, keep, invest. They repeat this cycle for however many times it takes until they achieve their goal of financial freedom. After that, it's up to them whether they want to relax or start taking on riskier investments. One day soon, that will be your reality too.

Rule #3: Millionaires Are Intentional about Their Time

One thing that millionaires are *very* good at is using their time effectively and efficiently. Time is the only nonrenewable resource and everyone has the same amount of it each day. Millionaires do their best to make sure that they're using every second as efficiently and effectively as they can.

To start, they often learn how to leverage their time by delegating time-consuming activities, which frees up their schedule for the big-picture things, like vision and strategy, as well as income-generating activities. A few of the things that millionaires hire out are yard chores, house cleaning, grocery shopping, running errands, cooking, bookkeeping, tax preparation, and other administrative tasks that don't require their brainpower—only their supervision.

With the time they get back from delegating those tasks, millionaires are able to invest in themselves *and* others. Their happiness also increases, because instead of spending time on the mundane, they can now focus on improving their lives in areas like:

- *Personal health,* such as mindset, sleep, nutrition, and exercise. Before the physical house you live in, your body is your first home. It makes sense that you run the best "hardware" and "software" (aka your mindset) available!
- *Experiences* that cultivate relationships, broaden their worldview, and spark innovative ideas.
- *Personal growth* through books, courses, and mentors that will expedite their path to success.
- *Personal networks* through masterminds, mentors, coaches, and meetups. As the saying goes, you are the average of the five people you spend the most time with, so it's important to choose these five wisely.
- *Giving back to the community* through contributing their time, knowledge, and/or money.

---

[7] Whitney Elkins-Hutten, "Millionaire Spending Habits to Master—No Matter Your Income," *Personal Finance* (blog), BiggerPockets, November 7, 2020, https://www.biggerpockets.com/blog/key-millionaire-spending-habits.

Your Path to Being an Everyday Millionaire

When I discovered these three rules about millionaire spending habits, a lot changed for me! Before I became a millionaire, I thought I needed to scrimp, save, and deprive myself to get there. But learning about millionaire spending habits really opened my eyes to the truth.

By following the rules outlined above, as well as sticking to the tried-and-tested cycle of creating, saving, and investing, you, too, will soon be on the path to creating financial freedom for yourself—whatever that may look like for you.

You have everything that you need to make yourself a millionaire. You don't need to be born into the right family or develop once-in-a-lifetime skills. You can learn everything you need to accomplish this.

The next two chapters in this section will be fun. We're finally going to talk numbers and strategies to see how you create a solid financial plan for yourself now and for generations to come.

═ YOUR CHAPTER ACTION PLAN ═

1. Journal about how you can apply Rule 1 in your life. When you think about spending money on your "needs" versus your "wants":
   - Where do you feel the most out of balance in your spending? (e.g., clothing, dining out, new cars, etc.)
   - When do you feel the most out of balance in your spending? (e.g., holidays, birthdays, when you're stressed out, etc.)
2. Journal about how you can apply Rule 2 in your life. When you think about how you create, keep, and grow your wealth:
   - Where do you see yourself initially needing the most support?
   - Who can help support you?
3. Journal about how you can apply Rule 3 in your life. When you think about how you spend your time:
   - What tasks or obligations can you cut entirely to free up time? If you don't need to do it, and it doesn't completely light you up, get rid of it.
   - What tasks can you automate to free up time? This could mean using technology or creating a simple checklist to get you through a task more quickly.
   - What tasks can you delegate to free up time? Even if you can't delegate a task yet, write up a process document to better automate the task now and in the future.

Real Stories of Money for Tomorrow
PRINCIPLES IN ACTION

Adrienne Green, Adrienne Green Realty

Have you ever felt great things were possible, yet your education didn't show you how to get there?

I knew I wanted financial freedom, but my business education wasn't moving the needle enough to make it happen. Then I learned about real estate investing and everything changed. I exceeded what I thought was possible, and I'm continuing to achieve more.

In 2007 I graduated from the University of Southern California with a bachelor's in business administration with a focus in finance. In terms of investing, my courses focused exclusively on the stock market. We worked through numerous studies that demonstrated the challenges of active management and how it was nearly impossible to truly beat the market. I was taught that average returns in the stock market were the way to build wealth. My first job out of college was with Western Asset Management Company, a bond fund manager. I was completely entrenched in the world of working for a big company and investing in the stock market.

Stock market investing was my sole strategy for five years, until 2012. That year my husband changed jobs from a traditional, larger corporation to a small business, where his coworkers were more "out of the box" thinkers. As people willing to work at a newer small business, they had greater risk tolerance, and several of his colleagues had rental properties. This was the first time we'd met people like us—not those who were already millionaires—who invested in real estate. This made my husband and I realize that we could supplement our income and diversify our investments with real estate. We also saw that we didn't necessarily have to do it in the sunset portion of our lives, when we would have accumulated the funding to start through years of traditional work and savings. We could start it soon!

An opportunity presented itself shortly after my husband switched jobs. We decided to move, and we thought that keeping our house as a rental would be our entry into real estate investing, yet as we evaluated that option, we saw it wasn't the best choice. There were several challenges due to our previous "traditional" saving and investing mindset. It would be a "premium offering," meaning higher vacancy rates affecting the income. Additionally, we had a fifteen-year mortgage on it, which made it difficult to cash flow. Finally, in terms of our personal finances, with all of the equity we had in the townhouse, and the down payment we were making for our new house, our finances would be tight if we kept it (and we wouldn't be maximizing leverage). We realized that as much as we wanted to start real estate investing, holding on to this town house as a rental wasn't a wise choice. So we sold, knowing another opportunity would come.

A few months after selling the house and moving into our new one, another opportunity for real estate investing presented itself! We realized that we could house hack our new home by creating a basement rental, as the space was sitting there empty and unused. It had its own entrance, a bedroom, a bathroom, and a common area where we could build out a kitchenette. Was it turnkey and ready to go when we bought this house? No. Could we take what we had and make it into something that would work? Yes.

Renting out that basement really took us outside of our comfort zone at the time, and our motivation to get passive income and build wealth kept us going. Everything about it seemed challenging: planning out the kitchen, getting the supplies, and then the weeks of constructing it in our free time! Once the physical space was ready, there was preparing the lease and learning about self-managing a rental. Plus, there was a lot of stress and nerves about having people in a part of our home. What if the people were loud? What if they didn't pay? It helped to know other people who had rental properties and to learn about their experience and that it worked out okay for them—so we would probably be fine. We posted the rental listing online and had it rented out to tenants within a couple of weeks. It went smoothly. Sure, sometimes they listened to the TV a little loudly, and we could hear it. Still, it was well worth the income!

The basement house hack went very well, and we realized it was the easiest money we were making. This prompted us to save up for the down payment to buy an investment property. Then we'd save up and do it again. As we gained experience, things got easier. Now my husband and I have around a dozen doors at any given time, and we've done various types of real estate investing: local and long-distance, short- and long-term rentals, flips, BRRRRs, syndications, and even an RV park.

As someone who went through business school and was trained to invest in the stock market, I'm still surprised that real estate investing wasn't discussed as a viable investment option. I'm so glad I learned about it and that we had the courage to give it a try. At the end of the day, the truth is in the numbers, and real estate investing has built transformational wealth for me and my family. Without it, we would be living a different life than we now enjoy. Real estate investing has enabled us to create a life and build more wealth than we had thought possible!

===== **CHAPTER 6** =====

Building Your Financial Moat

The best defense is a good offense.
—**GEORGE WASHINGTON**

Back in medieval times, people needed to be creative if they wanted to be able to protect what they held dear. And one of the ways they did this was by building moats around their buildings, fortifications, or towns.

The idea of moats was ingenious. They are wide, deep ditches dug around whatever area you want to protect. Sometimes they are dry, but usually they are filled with water. Back then, moats served as the first line of defense. Since most attacks were carried out on foot, a moat would drastically slow down the enemy's approach time, giving you time to prepare and ready your defense or prepare a counterattack.

Today, most people don't build actual moats. Instead, let's take the concept and apply it metaphorically to our finances. Let me introduce you to the concept of the *financial moat.* Similar to how moats represented the first line of defense for medieval cities, a financial moat will protect your wealth.

You see, we're not just building for the now. I've always been big on planning for the future, and I know we can make small changes in our lives that will benefit us in the long term. We want to set a foundation that will make it possible for you to keep your wealth within your family for generations. Additionally, creating a defense system for your finances will contribute to making your goals a reality, all while giving you unmatched peace of mind.

How will we create this financial moat?

Creating your financial moat boils down to two important things: personalized savings accounts and taking full advantage of your credit score. We're going to examine both of these in great detail to give you an idea of what a good financial moat should look like, as well as what you can start doing today to create your own.

Please note that what is contained in this chapter is more of a suggestion than a methodical guide. The savings rates and the recommendations are all dependent on your current financial situation. You can tailor them to suit your needs. The most important thing is getting started, not following what's written here word for word.

Your Three Must-Have Accounts

A lot of this book talks about investing. But saving or putting aside money in extremely low-risk savings accounts is imperative to strengthening your personal financial position. As with all things, it's about finding a balance—because what value is wealth if you can't access some of your money quickly in the event of an emergency or to fund the activities you wrote down during your Happiness Formula exercise?

After years of working with clients, and putting this into practice in my own life, I've realized that you need *three* accounts to help strengthen your financial future, as well as to make your life enjoyable now. They are an emergency account, a happiness account, and a wealth account.

The Emergency Account

Out of the three, the emergency account is the most important to start with if you don't already have one. Emergencies derail us from our financial goals if we don't have any money put aside "just in case." According to *Fortune* magazine, 57 percent of Americans can't afford a $1,000 emergency, and emergencies *will* happen.[8] You need to prepare for emergencies with an account to deal with any of the major expenses that may pop up. To avoid being overwhelmed with your savings goal, start off with just $1,000 and set a goal to grow it to three-to-twelve months' worth of expenses as soon as you can.

Notice the wide range. Your goal should be dependent on your situation. Let's look at two examples.

---

8 Ivana Pino, "57% of Americans can't afford a $1,000 emergency expense, says new report," *Fortune*, January 25, 2023, https://fortune.com/recommends/banking/57-percent-of-americans-cant-afford-a-1000-emergency-expense/.

If you have a lucrative job in an in-demand field, maybe three months is enough. You can find a job quickly if you ever get laid off. You don't have to worry so much about your bills, and you can tap into investments if necessary. But huge cash savings might not be the right move for you.

But that's not always the case. Maybe you have kids and a mortgage, debt to pay off, or multiple car payments. Maybe it would be harder for you to find another job in your field or maybe you're self-employed. Then saving up to twelve months would be more ideal.

My sweet spot is to set aside six months of expenses, plus all my insurance deductibles.

Everyone's number is going to be different. Ask yourself, *What will allow me to sleep well at night?* That's your number.

As soon as you set aside your first $1,000, you'll start to feel more secure. However, don't touch the money in this account! It's not free money for you to go shopping or take trips with. Only use it for emergencies. When an unexpected major expense happens, you'll be happy you decided to start saving for a rainy day.

The Happiness Account

The concept of the happiness account is setting aside money so you can say yes to experiences that will make you happy and enrich your life.

For this account, I like to start diverting with 3 percent of your gross income. If you earn $100,000 per year gross, then your happiness account should have $3,000 going into it each year, or around $250 per month. The account will grow as your income grows, even at just a 3 percent savings rate.

Now, 3 percent may not be earth-shattering money. But you're muscle-building. You're getting into the habit of setting something aside to fund your happiness now. As your passive income grows, you'll be able to set aside more and more money each year toward your happiness account.

My husband and I used the money set aside in our happiness account to cross a few events off our bucket list in 2022—seeing the Red Hot Chili Peppers, Elton John, and *Hamilton*, all live! This was in addition to our planned travels. We didn't have to think about where the money would come from when tour dates were announced, or if we were sabotaging our goals by splurging on these experiences, because we had funded an account specifically for those experiences.

Life is meant to be enjoyed! We don't want to deprive ourselves of what makes us happy to the point where we end up making decisions that ultimately sabotage our goals and investing plans.

The Wealth Account

This account is the money you will set aside and use to fund your future investments. The goal is to start by setting aside between 1 percent and 5 percent of your gross income, and then start increasing your savings rate by 1 percent per month for an entire year. That will get you bumped up to about a 12 percent to 17 percent savings rate per year, with minimal pain as you dial in on your value-based spending plan. This is where all the work you did on your balance sheet earlier starts to shine!

As you get more comfortable with your higher savings rate, it's important to not become complacent. Consider sticking with periodic increases to your savings rate until your savings rate is 20 percent or more. The money you set aside here will be used exclusively in support of investing and building your wealth. In Chapters 11 and 12, we will discuss how to invest and grow these funds in such a way that you can create your desired monthly passive cash flow. For now, know that the more you can save into your wealth account—and later invest—the more quickly you will reach your goal of financial freedom.

Where to Set Up Your Accounts

The next question you may have is where to set up these three accounts. For emergency and happiness accounts, I prefer to keep them in the same place: an FDIC-insured bank with great customer service, making it easy to access your money with low to no fees. You can check out NerdWallet's yearly review of banks to make a choice if you would like to hold your money somewhere other than your primary bank. It's also important to note that you shouldn't hold more than $250,000 per depositor per bank—that's the FDIC deposit insurance limit. If you have more than that in an account with a single bank , consider having multiple accounts at separate banks so your money will be insured.

Ideally, you want to keep your happiness and emergency accounts somewhere where you won't pay ATM fees, statement fees, or monthly maintenance fees. It would also be great if you could get a little bit of interest (as of this writing, 2 percent to 5 percent is reasonable) on these savings each year. Every cent counts. I also like to keep my happiness and emergency account in the same place. After fully funding your emergency account, you can sweep the extra into your happiness account.

Where you keep your wealth account depends on your long-term goals. If you're primarily focused on traditional retirement investing, then you can set up your accounts with your work—a 401(k), 403(b), or TSP. However, if you're more like me and don't necessarily want a standard retirement plan, you may opt for an all-cash investment plan in real estate and other assets. Or you may want more control over how you invest your retirement funds and prefer to go with a self-directed IRA provider. Of course, you could do a blend of both—saving some of your wealth in your retirement accounts and saving part to purchase assets directly. In either case, there are other options out there.

For now, if you remain undecided, you could put aside your income in a high-yield account at the same institution as your emergency and happiness accounts. However, if you decide to make the switch from a traditional retirement plan to an all-cash investment plan (say, in real estate), make sure you've considered *everything*. Not just the advantages, but also the potential risks of self-managing your retirement fund (or not funding retirement at all and just investing). Another place that I really love stashing money is a cash flow life insurance policy—it's outside the banking system, but it will still grow and you can utilize that to fund your wealth plan.

To end this section, I want you to put this book down right now and get on your computer to take action on what we've just discussed by following these five steps:

1. Research the best bank for your accounts,
2. Open an emergency savings account,
3. Open a happiness savings account,
4. Open a wealth savings account, and
5. Set up recurring deposits to each account.

It should only take you a few minutes, but it will be immensely worth it. Bonus points if you open these accounts at a different bank than you normally do business with. Why? This will make it harder for you to "dip" into these accounts for random (and often unnecessary) splurges. Rather, it will create just enough friction for you that you leave these monies untouched as you build toward your goals. Remember, these accounts will be your first line of financial defense, your very own financial moat.

Your Credit Score

The next part of shoring up your financial defenses involves maximizing your credit score. Depending on your previous experiences, you might be extremely excited to dive into this or a little nervous to discuss it.

I've found that all too often, the content surrounding credit scores is unnecessarily complicated or even too fear-inducing. It's my goal to demystify your credit score and see it for what it really is—a tool that can help you create financial freedom.

What Is a Credit Score?

Your credit score is a tool that is used to predict how likely you are to pay back a loan on time. It utilizes a scoring model and collects information from your credit report to assign you a number, or "score." It's primarily used by financial institutions, but even people like your landlord or your employer might have an interest in your credit score.

A number of things can influence your credit score, since credit reporting companies usually aggregate data from multiple places to ensure they have an accurate idea of your lending history. Some of these factors are:

- Your bill-paying history,
- Any unpaid debt you may have,
- The number of loan accounts you have,
- The type of loans that you take,
- How long you have had your loan accounts open,
- How much of your available credit you are using,
- Any new applications for credit made on your behalf, or
- Whether you have had a debt sent to collection, a foreclosure, an eviction, or a bankruptcy, and how long ago that event was.

Why Is Understanding Your Credit Score Important?

Financial institutions will use your credit score to determine your creditworthiness. It is what they use to decide if they should lend you money, how much to lend you (aka your credit limit), and how favorable the terms will be.

Credit scores fall into five ranges.

- Exceptional: 800–850
- Very Good: 740–799
- Good: 670–739
- Fair: 580–669
- Poor: Under 580

Without a credit score that at least falls into the Fair range, it will be hard to access a mortgage, credit card, auto loan, or other credit product you may need.

Credit scores also determine the interest rate you'll receive on a loan or credit card, and even the credit limit is subject to your credit score. Ideally, you want to have a higher credit score because it will make it easier for you to qualify for loans, better interest rates that will lower your expenses, and even jobs.

Once you know your credit score, you have leverage that you can use to further achieve your goals. Do you know your credit score? My favorite tool to use to determine your score is CreditKarma.com. This isn't an endorsement of their services, but it does make the whole process simpler. Credit Karma pulls all three reports from the leading reporting companies—Equifax, Transunion, and Experian—and even educates you on any credit changes you have had recently and how you can manage them.

However, Credit Karma isn't your only option. You can use any credit reporting agency of choice (Equifax, TransUnion, or Experian) and pull your report directly through them. You can get a free report each year from each credit reporting agency, or you can pay for their services if you'd like to see your score more frequently or get a more detailed report.

Your credit score might not be 100 percent accurate. Every now and then there may be discrepancies and issues—late payments that weren't actually late, paid-off loans or credit cards that haven't been updated as such, and even loans on your report that aren't yours or that should have been written off. I've even found reports where my name wasn't spelled correctly. You want to make sure you're checking that everything listed on your report is accurate. It's your job to advocate for yourself and ensure your credit report is factual and accurate.

I encourage all my clients to get more acquainted with their credit reports, as it's a tool you can use to your advantage. So, we're going to end this section with an exercise for you to get on top of this.

1. Open a CreditKarma.com account,
2. Review your account for any issues or discrepancies, and
3. Set a reminder on your calendar to review your account every quarter until all credit issues are resolved, and your score is where you want it to be.

Protecting Your Assets

What do you have in place for a freak accident? By now, we've all heard of what happened to Damar Hamlin, the American football safety who, in 2023, took a hit to the chest that caused him to have a massive heart attack. He ended up having to be resuscitated twice, once on the field and again in the hospital. Since then, he's made a remarkable, possibly one-in-a-million recovery, and might even be able to play football again.

But what if it hadn't happened like that? What happened to Damar can happen to any one of us, at any point on our quest to create wealth. When we think about generational wealth, we often think about wills that will execute our wishes *after* we've passed. But you should consider additional tools in the event you end up in a freak accident rendering you incapable of making decisions for yourself or even barring you from working again.

Following consultation with a legal professional, I would suggest implementing the following.

- An **advance healthcare directive**, also known as a **living will**, helps guard against a sudden change in your health condition draining your accounts. This set of legal documents includes a health care power of attorney, living will directives, and HIPAA authorization. Through these documents, you define what actions should be taken for your health if you are no longer able to make decisions for yourself due to illness or incapacity. If you become unconscious or mentally incompetent, a medical power of attorney allows you to appoint someone to make medical care decisions on your behalf. With a signed HIPAA authorization and living will directive, medical records will be accessible to your designated agent, and health care professionals will be able to speak with your designated agent to make informed decisions. This differs from a durable power of attorney, which allows your agent to make broad legal decisions on your behalf.

- A **durable power of attorney** allows your agent to make broad legal decisions on your behalf, such as legal, health, and financial transactions (including opening and closing bank accounts; buying or selling stocks; filing tax returns; buying or renewing insurance policies; and making health care decisions). Be sure to consult with your legal professional regarding the best way to draft a power of attorney and who to designate as your agent.

- **Cash flow life insurance** is a specifically structured whole life policy. The primary purpose isn't a death benefit, even though it does provide one. The policy is structured to allow you to stuff money in it, for the lowest premium possible, so it can grow tax-free and you can use it as your own bank. However, the death benefit can help insulate you from any mistakes you may have made as an investor.

These three things can greatly protect your wishes, family, and portfolio, and help ensure that your wealth is protected now and in the future. In Chapters 14 and 15, we'll touch more on other things you can do, like wills, living trusts, and training heirs.

Securing your financial future doesn't have to be scary or complicated. You can take a few intentional steps to ensure you've shored up your financial defenses and dug your financial moat.

Once you've reviewed this chapter and taken action, it's time to move on to the next chapter, where we'll review where most individuals lose their wealth, and how you can avoid their common pitfalls.

═══ YOUR CHAPTER ACTION PLAN ═══

1. Build your financial moat.
   - Determine how many months of expenses you need to save for in your emergency account in order to sleep well at night.
   - Determine your savings rate for your happiness account.
   - Determine your savings rate for your wealth account.
   - Research the best bank to hold your accounts (keeping no more than $250,000 in cash for any one depositor at any one bank).
   - Open an emergency savings account.
   - Open a happiness savings account.
   - Open a wealth savings account.
   - Set up recurring deposits to each account until fully funded.
2. Get familiar with your credit score.
   - Open a CreditKarma.com account.
   - Review your account for any issues or discrepancies.
   - Set a reminder on your calendar to review your account minimally every quarter until all credit issues are resolved and your score is where you want it to be.
3. Consult an estate attorney to draft:
   - Advanced medical directives, including a health care power of attorney, living will, and HIPAA authorization
   - Durable power of attorney
   - Cash flow life insurance, depending on your individual situation (we will talk more about trusts and wills in a later chapter)

Real Stories of Money for Tomorrow
PRINCIPLES IN ACTION

Investing with Your Kids—Erin Hudson, managing partner,
Quattro Capital

*Any fool can spend money. But to earn it and save it and defer
gratification—then you learn to value it differently.*
—MALCOLM GLADWELL

When I was growing up, terms like "ROI," "cash flow," and "retirement" were not
discussed around the dinner table. Like most people, my parents worked nine-to-
five jobs building someone else's dream, and I knew come hell or high water there
had to be a better way.

I went on to become a doctor, and while in practice, I began investing in single-family rental properties. I quickly discovered the mailbox money and the power
that comes from continually reinvesting. Within two years, I acquired twenty-six
rental properties. I would buy three for $100,000, then increase the price on two
and sell them for $100,000, allowing me to keep one for free! Then I would rinse
and repeat. It was both empowering and confidence-building, and I knew I needed
my kids to get a taste of the goodness. What better way than to show them how
to make money while you sleep?

So, I had the perfect idea: It was time to educate my daughter on assets versus
liabilities.

I said to her, "You know how you want to buy a car [liability] for your 16th birth-
day, Rylee? What if I could create an opportunity for you to buy a rental property
[asset] instead? You can drive my car, and I will sell you one of my rental properties
[a freebie] for $7,000 [the amount in the bank for her car.]"

Let's just say, after she fought the inner battle, she chose the rental property.
In four years, she doubled the value of the property, sold it, and took the proceeds
to invest in her first apartment building at the age of twenty-one. Fast-forward to
today, and that same apartment building is selling next month for a healthy profit,
and she will then repeat the process.

Well, what do you know—my fourteen- and sixteen-year-olds inquired about
how they, too, could get into the game of real estate. It just so happens that when
I buy properties, I'm strategic: There have to be multiple options of what can be
done on the property. In 2017, I bought five acres that included a beautiful high-end
home on it that would make for a perfect Airbnb. The fact that the property was
outside city limits on unrestricted land made it that much more desirable because
I knew it would be perfect for adding tiny homes down by the pond in due time.

And that is exactly what Taylor and Tyler did. They styled out their 8-by-20-foot shipping-container homes. The experiential stays took off like wildfire, and they are now making $1,500 a month on a $50,000 investment (a 36 percent ROI!). Sometimes you just have to think outside the box, literally.

So, you may wonder, do I just let the two have all of the money from the properties? Not this mama ... there is another lesson for them to learn here! Each must bring their quarterly spreadsheet with the breakout for the nights rented with the nightly rates for me to review. Then the total proceeds are divided: They each get to keep half, and Mom gets half for footing the bill for the operation. Of the amount they make, half goes into their savings as seed money for the next investment, and the other half is their spending money (food delivery, Amazon, etc.). Yes, it's a time suck for me, but it is an incredible teaching opportunity for them that is bound to serve them very well in the future.

What a gift it has been to not just give my kids money, but also to have them work for it, learn how to stretch a buck, and duplicate their seed money. They have learned that there is truly nothing better than your money making babies. This mama is on fire for equipping the next generation and teaching them how to intentionally create generational wealth.

CHAPTER 7

The Four Horsemen That Can Destroy Your Wealth Growth: Interest

When it comes to your wealth,
hope is not a strategy.

If keeping wealth were easy, we wouldn't see so many stories of millionaires (and even billionaires) who have lost all or a large part of their fortunes. Personally, I think protecting your assets might be even more difficult than creating wealth in the first place—especially if you don't have an understanding of the potential pitfalls or "landmines" that can blow up your portfolio.

I've taken the time to catalog the top four landmines that can destroy your finances. I like to refer to them as the Four Horsemen—aka the four things that can cause a financial apocalypse for you on your wealth journey.

The First Horseman: Interest

I'm going to go out on a limb and assume that you didn't expect the first potential landmine in your portfolio to be how much *interest you are paying.* After all, interest can be amazing—when it's being paid to you on your own investments. However, since a major part of creating wealth involves acquiring assets (often through loans that utilize interest in their repayment models), getting a deeper understanding of what interest is and how it can sneakily erode your wealth is imperative.

Interest is a key part of a loan—you can't get away from it. However, you could be losing money without even knowing it, especially if you're paying consumer interest on car loans, credit cards, or unsecured loans; unnecessarily high mortgage interest; or fees if you miss an interest payment.

The concept I'm about to share with you is one I learned from Chris Miles at Money Ripples.[9]

Understanding the interest on your debt, and what is productive interest versus destructive interest, is a game changer in securing your financial future. When you take on any kind of debt—a loan on an asset, a personal credit card, a mortgage, or a student loan—you want to understand if the interest that you pay on that loan will be detrimental to your portfolio.

You see, not all interest is bad. Some debt is more efficient than others, and it's figuring that out that will make all the difference. We want to make sure any debt you carry is the most efficient kind, and that it's actually good debt. How can you tell?

If you've previously consumed any content on financial literacy, then you'll probably think of Dave Ramsey's way of solving this problem: List all the debt that you have and pay off the one with the highest interest rate first.

Maybe a few decades ago, that advice would have been stellar. However, our financial landscape has matured, and you have a lot more to consider when evaluating a loan than just the interest rate. In fact, a high-interest rate loan could be efficient, depending on the payment term and the potential monthly (or quarterly) income produced by the asset secured by the loan.

Financial media has other suggestions. Two that come to mind are the debt snowball and the debt avalanche.

The debt snowball strategy involves ranking your debt payments from the lowest to the highest payment amount and then paying off the one with the smallest payment first. After doing that, you snowball your debt payments by adding the payment of the recently paid-off loan to the next one in line in an effort to pay the next debt off faster. You rinse and repeat until all debts are paid off. This strategy is more of a momentum-building strategy for getting out of debt.

---

9 Chris Miles, Money Ripples, https://moneyripples.com.

The debt avalanche strategy is very different. This involves making the minimum payment on every debt you have, and then using any remaining funds that you have after paying all expenses to put toward the debt with the highest interest rate. This allows you to reduce the amount of interest you pay in the long run, in addition to reducing the amount of time you spend in debt.

These ideas are *tactics*, and I'm not taking away from their value. Thousands of people have benefited from these tactics and changed their financial situation. However, neither of those situations actually helps us to understand which is the best debt to pay off first. The technique that I'm about to show you does just that.

Chris at Money Ripples calls it the Cash Flow Index, a concept he learned from Garrett Gunderson at the Wealth Factory.[10] The index comes up with a weighted number, allowing you to figure out just what kind of debt you have. In order to come up with that number, you need to divide the loan balance by the minimum monthly payment. Once you've done that, you can compare the number you get with the chart below to help you understand where it stands.

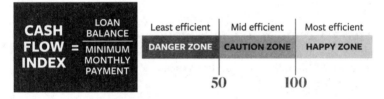

If the debt index number is 50 or below, then that debt is inefficient and eroding your portfolio. A debt with this index number is one you want to get rid of as quickly as you can. If the number you get is 100 or above, this debt is very efficient. In a case like that, it would be better to hold on to that debt and address other things before getting rid of it. If the number you get is between 50 and 100, you would want to make a note to restructure it. After you get rid of your danger-zone debt, you can then move on to your caution-zone debt.

Still a little confused? Don't worry! I've created a plan of action that you can follow to eliminate debt and start building wealth.

---

10 Garrett Gunderson, "How to Use the Cash Flow Index to Quickly and Safely Eliminate Your Debt," Wealth Factory, https://wealthfactory.com/articles/use-cash-flow-index-quickly-safely-eliminate-debt/.

Step 1: Calculate the Cash Flow Index for Each Debt You Carry

Log into your Empower.com account (or whichever account aggregator method you chose back in Chapter 3: Budgeting Is Dead) and make a detailed list of your debts. Note what is currently owed on them and include the minimum monthly payment for each.

Once you've got that information for all your debt, you need to calculate the cash flow index for each loan. Do this using the handy formula I mentioned above.

Loan Balance ÷ Minimum Monthly Payment = Cash Flow Index

The number you get will show you how effective that debt is at the given interest rate and payment term. A high number—anything over 100—means that your loan is efficient. A low number—anything under 50—means that your loan is inefficient.

Once you've got the Cash Flow Index for all your debt, let's move on to the next step.

Step 2: Create Your Game Plan

Now that you know what the Cash Flow Index of all your debt is, it's time to create a game plan. The first step is to put your debt in order from least efficient to most efficient.

Start with Your Least Efficient Debt

You'll want to start this process by evaluating the debt at the top of your list. Any debt with a Cash Flow Index of 50 or under is destructive to your wealth and is robbing you of money that could be better used to improve your financial situation. So, it's imperative to get rid of those debts as quickly as possible.

More often than not, you'll find that destructive debt (say, high credit card debt or monies owed to others) is a result of having destructive expenses like subscriptions you aren't using, purchases resulting from overspending, purchases related to abusive practices—like drugs, alcohol, or habitual shopping—and debt that is incurring fees (see Chapter 3 for a full list).

You'll want to make a plan to pay off these debts as soon as possible. You'll also want to eliminate the destructive habits tied to the destructive expenses so this type of debt doesn't reappear.

Figure Out What You Can Restructure

Any debt that falls between 50 and 99 is neither efficient nor inefficient, but there is plenty of room for optimization here! These debts are prime candidates for restructuring—or even elimination, depending on their terms and effect on your cash flow.

If the debt with this Cash Flow Index is consumer debt, then I would suggest eliminating it instead of restructuring it. You may also have the option to consolidate this type of debt with zero percent introductory APR credit lines, or a short-term loan with a zero percent interest rate. The goal would be to pay off your credit or loan balance before the zero percent interest rate expires, taking full advantage of the zero percent interest from whichever product you choose. (Warning: If you have problems using debt wisely, do not open more credit lines. It's best to just pay down the debt ASAP!)

If the debt is tied to a "potential" asset that is more of a "want" rather than a "need" for your investing strategy, consider if you really need to own the "asset" at all.

For example, a mentor of mine, Rich Fettke, was recently helping me think through a potential land deal. One of the questions he asked me was, "Do you need to own it to have it?" I sat silently for a minute, thinking through what my true intentions were with the land. The answer was a resounding NO! I just needed to *control the land through a lease*, not *own* it, to do what I wanted with it.

Additionally, you may choose to outsource some of your caution-zone debt to produce more cash flow for your bottom line—which is always a good way to create wealth. Some of the ideas that I have used with great success to turn caution-zone debt into efficient debt are renting out part of a home on Airbnb or VRBO, renting a camper on Outdoorsy, renting a car on Turo, renting a high-end mountain bike on Spinlister, and even renting a piece of land on Hipcamp.

Aside from restructuring, you can consider paying off the debt altogether. However, if the debt produces good cash flow, you have the options of renegotiating the interest rate with your lender to get the best term possible or completely refinancing the debt. These options are especially viable on real estate loans.

Decide How to Handle Your Efficient Debt

If any of your loans have a Cash Flow Index of 100 or higher, then it's operating pretty efficiently. Debt in this tier is less alarming than those in the other two buckets, but there are still ways you can maximize this kind of debt. Keep in mind that, while you may pick up small wins with restructuring the debt, you will need to consider the fees you would incur in order to restructure it. For some of my clients, they like to leave their efficient debt in place until they've tackled other debts—especially if it's tied to an income-generating asset.

Understanding the Interest You Are Paying Is Key

Yes, interest is one of the Four Horsemen and can destroy your portfolio, eroding your wealth—but understanding it through the lens of the Cash Flow Index math gives you massive control over your financial future.

When I first began my journey to financial independence, I was confused about which debt to eliminate first. I was following Dave Ramsey's popular debt snowball approach that I mentioned above, but it wasn't working out that well for me. That method didn't help me gain much momentum, and I ended up getting denied for a loan—even though I had a 680-plus credit score—simply because I didn't have enough cash flow coming in to make the bank feel comfortable lending to me.

But after implementing the plan I outlined above, utilizing the Cash Flow Index, I was able to eliminate all of my consumer debt, restructure my mid-tier debt to free up my cash flow, lower my debt-to-income ratio, and boost my savings and credit score significantly. I became *way more* attractive to lenders in just four months.

Paying interest on inefficient debt is a heavy weight on your finances and can drag down your wealth-building potential. So let's look at your action plan for this chapter before we move on to the next horseman.

═══ YOUR CHAPTER ACTION PLAN ═══

1. Calculate the Cash Flow Index for each debt your carry to see how interest might be eroding your wealth.
2. Create a game plan to eliminate any danger-zone debt, and reduce/renegotiate any caution-zone debt.

=== CHAPTER 8 ===

The Second Horseman: Insurance

The best we can do is size up the chances, calculate the risks involved, estimate our ability to deal with them, and then make our plans with confidence.

—HENRY FORD

The second horseman eroding your wealth is *insurance*. I know this must come as a surprise. After all, how can insurance end up having a negative outcome? At first glance, insurance seems like a simple, easy-to-comprehend tool—but just like interest, truly *understanding* it is critical to ensuring that you don't fall victim to this horseman.

The main goal of insurance is to outsource risk and liability. You pay a monthly (or yearly) fee for your policies so that if something goes wrong, and you pay the deductible, you're not on the hook for the remaining part of the bill. If you get into a car accident, your car insurance ensures you don't have to pay for the repairs or medical bills. If there's a fire, having homeowner's insurance means you don't have to pay to have your home renovated and your furniture replaced. It's a great tool that, when used properly, can be extremely beneficial to protecting your wealth building. But it's a bit like a double-edged sword—it can be just as destructive if you don't use it properly.

Personally, I love insurance policies! I get them for everything that I want to outsource my risk on—car, home, rental real estate, health, disability, life—if you can name it, I probably have a policy for it. So, this section isn't about trash-talking insurance companies. I want make sure you aren't wasting money on your insurance policies. The thing with insurance is *you want to get the best policy, without overpaying.* It's not about the cheapest price, but the *best* policy for the price.

Here are the three things you want to evaluate.

- *Ensure you're not paying for junk policies.* You might be signed up for an insurance policy that doesn't actually cover your risk or covers something that you no longer own or no longer use. It's a good idea to review all your policies once a year to find out what they cover and ensure that you don't have a junk policy or two sucking a few hundred dollars from you every month. An example would be a 25-year-old with no history or family history of cancer paying for a cancer insurance policy. Or someone paying for high-end vision and orthodontic insurance when they don't wear glasses and have perfectly straight teeth. Even paying for insurance on your appliances and cellphone when you could just stash a few hundred dollars in a high-interest bank account and self-insure your risk falls into this category.

- *Ensure that you don't have duplicate policies.* I know this sounds like a no-brainer, but I've seen it happen to so many of my clients. Sometimes, people might end up with two insurance policies on their car, or have the same item insured for the same kind of coverage with two different companies (yes, this includes warranties on appliances, cars, and technology!). Audit your insurance policies frequently to make sure you don't have any duplicates.

- *Ensure you're not overpaying.* Research is your friend in this instance. Shop around to see if other companies offer the same kind of coverage you have for less. I've found it's so easy to get so wrapped up in the personal relationship with the salesperson who sold you your first policy that you don't actually check to ensure you're getting the best deal. (Be sure to read the fine print if you think you've found what you have for less somewhere else; triple-check before you make your decision.)

I fell into the trap of a less-than-ideal insurance policy once. When I was working with a financial coach several years ago, I decided to take a look at what I was paying for insurance coverage. By the time I was finished weeding out junk policies, duplicate policies, and plain-and-simple overpriced coverage, I ended up with over $1,497 in annual savings. While that might not seem like a lot on its own, if I were to invest my savings of $1,497 each year and allowed that money to compound annually at 7 percent for 30 years, I would have $151,953!

Yes, by simply taking stock of my insurance coverage, I was, all of a sudden, nearly $150,000 closer to financial independence—and I could get there without sacrificing my lifestyle. That's why I want you to take the time to look through what you're paying for. There are a few facts about the insurance industry that these big companies don't want you to know.

- *The warranties that companies sell you are more lucrative than the items themselves.* So few people actually utilize their warranties, and these companies tack on a "minimal" amount of money to the sales price per month which, over time, allows them to make more than they did selling you the item. If you're worried about your new appliance or phone giving out after a few months or years, put aside some money in your emergency account to take care of any issues that may arise. When you keep money in your control, you're the one earning interest on it. Plus, if the worst doesn't happen, it's yours to put toward your financial goals.

- *You can shop around for a new policy at almost any time.* This one feels a little underhanded, I know, especially if you've built up a relationship with your insurance company. But you don't need to wait for a renewal to come up to change your policy. You can source a new policy at any time, and then cancel the old policy. The only thing this may not apply to is life insurance.

- *Grouping policies with one insurance vendor to get a discount isn't always cheaper.* Even though insurance companies want you to think this is true, it's not. Grouping your car, home, and health insurance might be more convenient for you, but it certainly isn't always cheaper. By separating them, you could end up saving yourself hundreds of dollars per month—allowing you to sock away tens of thousands toward your investing plan. Companies are usually good at insuring just one thing, but having them insure *everything* is the quickest way to overpay for your policies. (I ended up saving over $800 per year when I left a vendor who was offering me a "group discount" and instead chose the best companies to insure my car, home, and term life).

As a self-professed lover of insurance, I have some tips to share about how you can outsource as much liability as possible *and* save money while doing it.

The first tip—and the first step—is to sit down with a qualified insurance broker and consider your options for optimizing your coverage.

Here are my remaining tips about insurance, categorized by type. As a disclaimer, I'm not an agent; this is what I've learned over the years.

Health Insurance

- **Use the health coverage your employer provides.** In most cases, this is easily the most cost-effective way to secure comprehensive health insurance. A group policy with your employer—if this is an option for you—allows the cost to be split among a large group of people, making it cheaper than if you purchased health insurance on your own. If you are comparing two employment opportunities, it is worthwhile to factor in the benefits of the health insurance plans in your overall compensation. Getting affordable health insurance coverage can be difficult—it's not entirely unheard of for someone to take on part-time work just to get coverage for their needs.
- **Consider high-deductible insurance or self-insure.** If you're relatively healthy, this will make sure you get the best value for your money, since most of your expenses will be minor. If you aren't a super healthy individual, securing the best health coverage possible is a good idea.
- **Put away money in a health savings account (HSA).** Using a high-deductible plan will also give you the opportunity to set aside funds into a health savings account. Once your account balance reaches a certain level, you can even invest it. Health savings accounts can also be self-directed, which is an added bonus.

Disability Insurance

- **Know what your coverage entails.** You're basically insuring your ability to earn an income. Be aware, as there are differences in the types of policies. Some policies cover if you can't work *your own* occupation anymore. Other policies cover if you can't work *any* occupation anymore. Be sure to talk to a specialist about which type of policy is best for you.

Automobile Insurance

- **Think about a high-deductible auto policy.** Auto insurance is another area where you can secure a higher-deductible policy and self-insure for minor expenses unless there is an extenuating need. For example, I just renegotiated my automobile and travel trailer policies. It made sense for me to slightly bump up my deductible per vehicle/trailer, but I saved $600 per year doing so and put that cash in the bank to earn interest to help me pay the higher deductible. I'm actually earning money in this instance, rather than paying more.

- **It's safer to get more than you need here.** Since auto insurance is the most likely to be used of all policies, the key to auto insurance is not to be underinsured on liability, uninsured/underinsured motorist, or medical pay. Having been in a bad car wreck where the other driver was not insured, I can safely say you will be glad to have adequate coverage!

Homeowner's Insurance/Renter's Insurance

- **A high-deductible policy could work here as well.** To optimize cash flow, consider getting a high-deductible policy and self-insure for minor expenses. Don't forget your homeowner's policy also covers your personal possessions up to a specific dollar amount. So, it's a good idea to video-document all of your belongings and save your receipts for large-ticket items. In addition, your homeowner's policy may not cover collectibles like jewelry and art. Be sure to add any additional policy riders if you need that type of coverage.

- **Ensure you're adequately insured.** As the cost of materials and labor rises, be sure to check in periodically with your coverage provider to make sure your homeowner's policy coverage is still adequate should you sustain a catastrophic loss. In December 2021, our community lost more than 1,100 homes due to a fast-moving urban fire, and many homeowners found themselves grossly underinsured to rebuild their homes. For example, they may have insured their home at purchase in 2011 at a replacement cost of $200,00. However, the same home in 2021 costs $375,000 to rebuild. Many people are unable to close a $175,000 shortfall to rebuild their home if they stick with their initial insured replacement cost. I revisit my coverage every couple of years. You don't want to be sweating should a disaster strike!

- **Make sure your home office is covered.** If you have a home office, make sure you are covered for the loss of your home office and work production should you sustain a loss. Many home insurance policies either don't cover a home office at all or limit coverage (say, to $2,500) the second any personal equipment is used in a business capacity. If you don't see clients in your home, the best course of action is to ask your insurer for a home business insurance coverage endorsement. If you see clients in your home, it's best to get a separate business policy altogether.
- **Make sure you're covered if you're a renter.** If you don't own a home, be sure to secure a quality renter's policy to insure your belongings, as your landlord's homeowner's policy most likely won't cover any of your losses. Keep in mind that most residential leases exclude the rental from business use, so make sure you have adequate business coverage if you have a home office and are renting.

Umbrella Insurance

- **This kind of coverage is worth the investment when structured properly.** An umbrella policy provides protection beyond other policies' coverage limits. Umbrella policies are relatively inexpensive and worth the investment if you have significant assets or are looking to protect yourself from costly liability claims, especially if your assets exceed your auto or home liability insurance limits.
- **Use umbrella insurance to fill in your gaps in coverage.** This is a great way to coordinate other insurance policies together to fill in gaps in liability on home and auto. Be sure the underlying liability policy meets the terms of the umbrella policy.

Life Insurance

You need life insurance, no matter what you think. Experts will advise clients that they only need insurance if they are married, have one or more children, are the primary income earner in the household, have a dependent with special needs, owe debts (business, student loans, car loan, mortgage, etc.), or want to leave behind money to pay for burial expenses.

However, I firmly believe *everyone* should have some life insurance, as it helps you insure your life value, even if you are a homemaker. The proceeds from a life insurance policy can also help smooth the financial transition for your loved ones in the event of your untimely death. Think of insurance as a family guard dog—you hope you never need your guard dog to do his thing, but you are more than glad you have him around the house just in case. There are a couple of different types of life insurance: term life and permanent life.

- **Term life insurance** is a life insurance policy that has a set premium that remains the same throughout a set period of time. If you get a twenty-year policy, you are covered for twenty years. Should you die during those twenty years, a life insurance payout is paid to your beneficiaries (the people you picked to receive the death benefit of your policy). For example, if you buy a $300,000 policy with a twenty-year term and die within that time period, your beneficiaries would receive $300,000. This type of policy is generally inexpensive when you are young and only provides a death benefit.

- **Permanent life insurance** policies give you coverage for life, and the premiums you pay help to build a cash account. This greater value accumulates tax-free, allowing its holder to borrow against it with tax advantages or access it during their lifetime. With time, this account can grow into a significant asset that can provide funding for retirement. There are two different types of permanent life insurance: whole life and universal.
  - With **universal life insurance**, there can be a variation in premiums and death benefit. Due to the premium flexibility, the projected future guaranteed cash value may change during the course of coverage despite having a guaranteed interest rate.
  - With **whole life insurance**, the premium payments never change or increase with age, so you always know the cost. There is also a guaranteed death benefit. If designed right, the cash value can grow in a few short years and is guaranteed. The cash value can be used for an emergency fund, your own personal bank, or generating an arbitraged return when investing.

Either of these two options, term life or permanent life, would be instrumental in helping you protect and grow generational wealth.

Case in point: In 2005, my father passed away after exhausting two health insurance policies and a disability policy due to his medical conditions (conditions that are unfortunately becoming more common every day). From the outside looking in, you may have thought our family was going into bankruptcy, not only due to the loss of my father's high-income paycheck, but also the crushing medical and long-term care debt he was racking up. But my father had a whole life insurance policy that was paid up, and when he passed, the proceeds from the policy paid off his remaining debts and left a small nest egg for my mother to begin rebuilding her life.

But even before that happened, I learned just how important insurance is in a very personal way. In 2000, my life could've been upended if it weren't for insurance—I was hit by a drunk driver. The wreck was terrible; my friend (who was also in the car) and I ended up with serious injuries. My back was broken, I couldn't work, and the driver who hit us didn't have automobile insurance.

Fortunately, the medical pay on my auto insurance, my health insurance, and my disability insurance all kicked in to ensure my medical bills were paid, and I still had income coming in. In 1999, my out-of-pocket deductibles for all three insurance policies totaled $3,000: $2,000 medical deductible, $500 auto deductible, and $500 disability deductible. Now, $3,000 was about 8 percent of my take-home salary at that point in time. However, I was extremely happy to cap my out-of-pocket expenses to just that! Otherwise, this situation could have put me in a sticky financial situation with at least $15,000 in lost wages and another $50,000-plus in medical bills. More importantly, I would not have been able to focus on my recovery—which took about four months—if I didn't have insurance and was left wondering how to dig myself out of a financial hole.

And this isn't the only time insurance has saved my proverbial financial rear end. In 2017, our health insurance covered my husband's emergency appendectomy. In 2018 and 2022, our health insurance covered my husband's injuries from two separate mountain bike wrecks. In 2021, our health insurance covered my emergency surgery to treat a septic infection from a botched urgent care visit. In 2023, our health insurance covered the emergency room and ongoing orthopedic care for our daughter when she broke her thumb. And the list goes on. Keep in mind, all of these situations were simple accidents and injuries from living life, and our insurance safeguarded us from crippling medical costs.

In the end, I just want you to have peace of mind and protection. The right insurance policies are a must-have to outsource liability and protect your wealth, and with these tips, you'll be able to wield this tool effectively without falling victim to this horseman.

YOUR CHAPTER ACTION PLAN

1. Review and optimize how you are using insurance to outsource liability:
   - Health
   - Disability
   - Automobile
   - Homeowner's/renter's
   - Umbrella
   - Life
2. Consider opening a whole life insurance policy specifically designed to build your own personal "bank."

CHAPTER 9

The Third Horseman: Fees

If you don't have a plan for your money,
I guarantee someone else does.

This horseman can be particularly dangerous because fees are generally *hidden*. Yes, banks, credit card companies, investment firms, and even retirement advisors/fiduciaries all have fees baked into their services you might not know about. They could be costing you tens of thousands of dollars (probably hundreds of thousands of dollars) over the life of your portfolio.

I'm sure you've heard the saying "It's not what you make, it's what you keep." Yes, you can apply this saying to savings and investments, but also to fees. Fees snatch up money that could otherwise be put toward your financial freedom. And to illustrate just how detrimental fees can be, I want to show you an example using the fees that are arguably the most destructive: retirement fees.

Let's assume that the person in this example is forty-four years old. They have twenty-three years until their retirement, and they are putting away $20,500 per year into their company 401(k) with zero match from their employer. They are getting an average of 7 percent growth per year on their portfolio, which is reasonable, since historically the S&P 500 has grown on average by that amount.

Now, this person pays 1.50 percent in investment fees—a combination of what they pay for stocks, bonds, and mutual funds, as well as what their 401(k) fiduciary charges for the management of their portfolio. This is quite a moderate estimate since the combined fee in the real world is often closer to 2 percent.

■ Contributions **$666,090**　　■ Earnings **$527,775**　　☐ Total Fees **$228,014**

With these assumptions, *because of the fees*, this person ends up losing 30 percent of their portfolio (or over $228,000) by the time they are ready to retire. How come? Because you pay the fees (as a percentage of your account balance) regardless of how you actually do in the market. It doesn't matter if you make money or lose money—you always pay the fee regardless of how your investments perform.

But what if this person was savvy and able to reduce their overall plan and investment fees to 0.50 percent? As you can see below, they have reduced their fee load by 29 percent and have saved over $146,634 in fees and redirected that back into the earning power of their portfolio. In this model, they will retire with over $674,409 rather than $527,775—a $146,634 increase.

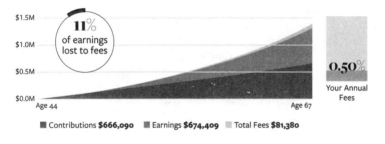

■ Contributions **$666,090**　　■ Earnings **$674,409**　　☐ Total Fees **$81,380**

Do you see why I think this is one of the most dangerous horsemen that you can fall victim to?

The most common pushback I get from my clients is, "I'm okay with some fees because I'm getting a company match." Well, let's play this out, and see if that is a good position to take.

Let's say instead of reducing their overall fees in their portfolio from 1.50 percent to 0.50 percent, our hypothetical person decides to change jobs and work for an employer that offers up to a $6,000 401(k) match annually on their funds invested for retirement. Nothing else changes about their situation (i.e., they are still paying 1.50 percent in total fees).

As you can see below, they still end up losing 30 percent of their portfolio (or over $294,000) to fees and generate about $150,000 more to retire on (similar results to the scenario where they just reduced their fees entirely).

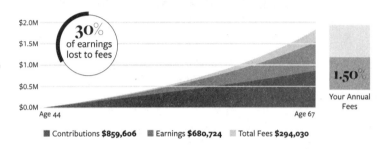

A better situation this person could put themselves in is to switch to an employer that offers a 401(k) match with low fees. As you can see below, this situation significantly decreases their expenses across the portfolio from 30 percent to 11 percent, allowing those funds to stay invested and grow—an additional $189,092 in growth!

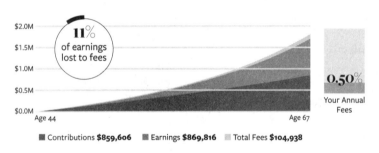

You don't want to get to your retirement age and end up realizing the "negligible" fees you paid during your working years ended up costing you such a sizable portion of your wealth.

However, the role of fees for most people is much worse. If we adjust the examples above to match the demographic of your average thirty-something-year-old, the dollar value of the money they stand to lose to fees skyrockets to over $500,000. Surely one would notice $500,000 missing from their accounts, right?

Wrong. If the loss happens in small amounts over thirty years, it becomes much harder to identify and track. Fees erode your future earning potential as well. As we saw above, if you are receiving a company match, that match actually incurs more fees, making things potentially worse, not better, in the long run. I know, because up until 2016 I was the unsuspecting person squirreling away money into my investment accounts, unaware of how much money these fees were actually taking from me in the long run.

So, how can you combat this horseman? Well, more than a decade ago, I adopted a two-step process to help eliminate those pesky fees from my portfolio—retirement fees and otherwise. I learned some great lessons along the way too, which I am going to share with you.

Step 1: Research the Fees You're Paying

Research your fees. I mean *all* the fees—not just the ones you know of. I want you to do a deep dive into your financial situation, and examine your transaction history and statements with a fine-tooth comb to find the areas where you might be leaking money to unnecessary fees. Here are a few categories to consider.

Bank Account Fees

These are probably the fees you're most aware of and are likely the most inexpensive. This includes account maintenance fees, checking fees, statement fees, overdraft fees, and ATM fees. Though they might not be that much, they add up over time. These kinds of fees will be posted on the bank website, or you can contact your branch manager for a list of these fees. Consider switching to a fee-free online bank to house your money, as long as they're FDIC insured and can keep your money safe.

Transaction Fees on Credit Cards and Loans

All loans and credit card instruments have transaction fees—even student loans, car loans, and property loans. These include everything from application fees to annual fees, transaction fees, and origination fees, and even fees used to buy down the rate, prepayment penalties, and junk fees.

All of these different kinds of fees add up quickly over time. While on their own they might not destroy your wealth, you will lose the compounded growth on all that money, which could be better used in building your wealth. It's a bit like the example I mentioned above—losing even a couple thousand dollars per year ends up costing you tens of thousands of dollars down the line.

In order to find these fees, you need to take a look at the contracts and fine print associated with these instruments. Companies are required by law to disclose this to you, so be sure to take a good look at the documents they present to you.

Investment and Retirement Fees

So many people fall victim to unnecessary, exorbitant fees in this area. There are *many* fees and expenses associated with retirement accounts, including but not limited to an expense ratio of 0.25 percent to 1.50 percent, sales load (front- and/or back-end loads), redemption fees, exchange fees, purchase fees, account fees, distribution fees, management fees that are on average 1.4 percent, and plan administration fees that are anywhere between 1 percent and 5 percent.

I definitely recommend visiting the Department of Labor website[11] and taking a look at their glossary explaining all the investment-related fees to see if there's anything you're paying for that may have flown over your head. Each year your company retirement plan has to file a Form 5500 with the Department of Labor. If you want to know what your exact fees are for your retirement plan, you can visit the Department of Labor's Form 5500 Search website. I would say that investment and retirement fees are the most dangerous to leave unchecked. They erode your wealth and are a ticking time bomb in your investment and retirement accounts.

And the fact that they are so freaking hard to research, despite having the largest impact on your accounts, is something else you have to be prepared for. In order to get to the bottom of all the fees you're paying, your best bet is to contact your benefits manager, your plan administrator, or your brokerage for a full list of the fees you're paying for your accounts.

Once you've taken stock of all the places where you might be leaking money, it's time to move on to the next step.

---

11 "Understanding Your Retirement Plan Fees," Department of Labor, https://www. dol.gov/agencies/ ebsa/about-ebsa/our-activities/resource-center/publications/ understanding-your-retirement-plan-fees.

Step 2: Eliminate or Reduce as Many Fees as Possible

Some of these fees may be more difficult to get rid of than others, so I've put together a few tips that you can use to reduce or eliminate each type of fee. Be sure to keep an open mind as you read these suggestions, as you need to examine *all* your options.

Reduce Bank Account Fees

If you're being charged more fees than necessary, or a fee for every single thing, then it's probably time to consider changing banks. You'll want to go with one that has free checking, no statement fees, low or no overdraft fees, and reimburses your ATM fees. Yes, switching banks might be a little tedious, but it's definitely worth it in the end. Your portfolio will thank you!

Check out NerdWallet's yearly roundup of the best banks and credit unions to see what's available. You can visit their website to get a better understanding of where you could be saving money to avoid the smaller charges adding up over time.

As a point of caution, however, if you do decide to move banks, take care to keep your total deposits with the bank under $250,000 per depositor (i.e., per social security number or EIN), which is the current FDIC insurance coverage level. Otherwise, your money won't be entirely insured—which is never a good thing.

Reduce Transaction Fees on Credit Cards and Loans

Before you get *any* line of credit, you need to compare and negotiate the application fees, annual fees, transaction fees, origination fees, points to buy down the rate, prepayment penalties, and junk fees whenever you can. You can also negotiate these fees after you already have the credit card or loan, though your chance of success in getting them reduced might be lower.

I like to compare the best program from at least three lenders. You can sometimes get a deal if you negotiate between lenders for your business. In fact, I recently did this in 2022 with a property loan and got a deal that was 0.5 percent under the going rate with $0 points. This will keep your transaction costs as low as possible.

Reduce Investment and Retirement Fees

Not only are investment and retirement fees the biggest pitfalls that can cost you the most money, but they are also some of the most difficult to eliminate or negotiate. With this in mind, sometimes the only way to keep more of your money is to opt out of the "system" entirely, and then find a better option to build your wealth—in a more controlled environment, on your terms. Here are some things to consider based on your situation:

- *If you have a 401(k) with your current employer,* you are kinda stuck paying the fees for the plan. However, you have the ability to choose investments that perform well and have a low expense ratio. As such, you should be sure to review your 401(k) every year at open enrollment to find out what fees you are paying compared to your employer. Believe it or not, employers can shift fees to you as long as they disclose them—even in teeny-tiny fine print.

- *If you have separated employment (i.e., you get fired or resign),* you can roll your portfolio over to a brokerage and/or a self-directed IRA. Yes, you can do both. While you might have the option to roll your account over to your new employer, keep in mind that you are locking those funds up in another 401(k) that you don't have true control over. You can have a brokerage IRA (funded by your old 401(k)) and a new 401(k) with your new employer if you desire. This keeps at least part of your retirement within your control.

I want you to analyze your portfolio with this in mind. You can log in to your Empower.com account and use the Retirement Fee Analyzer tool to create a model of the impact of fees on your portfolio (like our hypothetical employee above). Knowledge is potential power!

The truth is, finding and eliminating fees isn't as sexy as the other things you can do to build wealth. However, it's imperative and, to be honest, if you don't do anything else, you should definitely do this. It supercharges your ability to build wealth.

Because this is the scary truth—if you don't have a plan for your money, I guarantee that someone else does.

═══ YOUR CHAPTER ACTION PLAN ═══

1. Research your fees to see how they might be eroding your wealth.
2. Eliminate and/or reduce as many fees as possible.

CHAPTER 10

The Fourth Horseman: Taxes

> *I don't blame or complain about things like the economy, the government, taxes, employees, gas prices, or any of the external things that I don't have control over. The only thing I have control over is my response to these things.*
>
> **—JACK CANFIELD**

Are you surprised to see this heading? I don't think so. The topic of taxes can be polarizing, and if you're self-employed or own a business, taxes may be your biggest expense. When I first started on my wealth journey, I was delighted to know that investing in real estate could offset some of my tax burdens.

For example, depreciation can help you shelter your passive income (and possibly even your active income) from your rentals. Also, using a 1031 exchange when you sell a property could help you defer your depreciation recapture and tax on capital gains. You could even remove equity from your rentals tax-free through a refinance and invest in more property. You can use tax code in your favor; you just have to know how.

Before we get into this, I want to make it clear that this section isn't about refusing to pay what you legally owe—it's the opposite, actually. We're going to talk about how choosing *not* to legally reduce your tax burden will end up *costing you wealth* in the future. As a matter of fact, it's best described in the landmark Supreme Court decision *Gregory v.*

Helvering, where it was stated:

"Anyone may so arrange his affairs that his taxes shall be as low as possible; he is not bound to choose that pattern which will best pay the Treasury; there is not even a patriotic duty to increase one's taxes."[12]

It is your legal right to arrange your affairs so that your taxes will *legally* end up being as low as possible. And Tom Wheelwright, in my favorite book of his, entitled *Tax-Free Wealth*, breaks down the way to do this into five easy steps. I'm going to share those steps with you because they blew my mind when I discovered them.

I knew zilch about strategically reducing my tax bill when I first started investing. As a matter of fact, I think we're conditioned to pay taxes until we die. I was raised to go to school, get a great job, buy a house, get married, start a family, and contribute to my 401(k). With this kind of conditioning, the only way to reduce your tax burden was to take a standard deduction, deduct your mortgage interest (if you could), get a tax credit for being a good saver and possibly for your kids, defer your income until retirement, and hope the tax rate would be low by the time you were ready to retire.

Yet, even if you do this and the tax rate drops (and most of us in the U.S. are now realizing the tax rate most likely won't drop), you would still end up paying tens of thousands of dollars in taxes.

Hope isn't a strategy, though. That's why discovering Tom's five-step process felt so amazing. The process is a concrete, tangible, and *effective* way to lower your tax burden.

Before we get into it, I'd like to point out that I'm not a CPA, accountant, or tax guru. As with any advice, please consult a qualified tax strategist to understand how the information I'm about to share with you can apply to your unique situation.

There are two facts that I can share with you about taxes, though.

First, there is a clear order of operations you should follow to maximize your tax savings. The traditional narrative we grew up with is not the correct strategy if you're trying to significantly reduce your tax bill. The more you can save on your taxes today means more that you have to invest for tomorrow, allowing you to grow your wealth faster. Now that is maximizing the time value of money!

Second, the U.S. tax code is actually a treasure map telling us where

---

12 Ariel Gamburg, "How to Legally Minimize Your Tax Expenses to Increase Your Bottom Line," *Forbes*, September 4, 2018, https://www.forbes.com/sites/forbesnycouncil/2018/09/14/how-to-legally-minimize-your-tax-expenses-to-increase-your-bottom-line.

to invest our dollars. Real estate and business are two spaces where the IRS wants the private sector to solve problems. As a result, investors and business owners get the best tax breaks.

And that's the secret that the wealthy use to stay wealthy—they combine a clear strategy with the tax code's treasure map to reduce their tax burden!

Let's dive into how you can do the same.

Step 1: Take Deductions (Including Depreciation)

Deductions can reduce your taxable income by the percentage of your highest federal income tax bracket. If you fall into the 22 percent tax bracket, $10,000 of deductions saves you $2,200. But how can you accumulate $10,000 of deductions if you are a W-2 employee?

Investing in a business (even if you have just one rental property) allows you to be able to take deductions. It's one of the reasons why it's so important for you to move from an employee or self-employed to the business owner and investor side of the cash flow quadrant.

Some of these tax-deductible expenses include but are not limited to:
- Interest
- Depreciation
- Taxes
- Insurance
- Repairs and Maintenance
- Property Management Fees
- Utilities (Gas, Electric, Water, Phone, etc.)
- HOA Fees
- Professional Fees
- Snow Removal/Landscaping
- Travel Expenses
- Supplies
- Leasing Commissions
- Advertising/Marketing
- Business Mileage
- Education
- Bank Fees
- Employees and Independent Contractors
- Home Office Expenses
- Business Meals

The most significant deduction, which is borderline magical, is depreciation. Depreciation is simply an accounting method used to allocate the cost of a tangible or physical asset over the cost of its useful life. The IRS understands that tangible assets (such as real estate) will break down over time. At some point, the carpet, cabinets, and HVAC will need to be replaced. In their eyes, it would be best if you, as an investor, keep the asset in good working order. Therefore, the gift of depreciation is awarded to help us offset costs and reinvest back into the property. You could also use passive depreciation to shelter passive income and keep it tax-free.

A Note About Depreciation

I wholeheartedly believe depreciation is one of the largest and most accessible tax shelters out there. Yes, this may sound like a bold statement—but the math is on my side! And *anyone* can benefit from it; you don't have to be running a huge business.

The IRS actually wants you, as a business owner, to take advantage of depreciation. In fact, you're penalized if you don't. Currently, there are two ways that you can access depreciation, and both of them are accounting methods. They are:

- **Straight-Line Depreciation:** This is the simplest method for calculating depreciation over time. With this method, the same amount of depreciation is deducted each year from the value of an asset (a single-family, multifamily, or commercial building, for example) throughout the course of its useful life. Each type of asset has a different time frame for what qualifies as "useful life."
- **Accelerated Depreciation:** This one is a bit more complex. You'll still end up taking the same amount of depreciation over time as you would with the straight-line method. However, instead of breaking the depreciation into equal parts throughout the useful life of the asset, you take more depreciation within the first five years and less in the later years. This is done through a cost segregation analysis (CSA) identifying all the property-related costs that can be depreciated in under twenty years.

How can both of these methods be used for you? Let's say you buy a residential property for $1 million, and $200,000 of it is land value. You can't depreciate land, since it doesn't break down. However, you can depreciate the rest of the value—around $800,000—for the useful life of the residential property, which would be 27.5 years, according to the IRS.

This situation would give you two options:

- Straight-line depreciation of $29,000 per year for 27.5 years.
  - $800,000 ÷ 27.5 years = $29,000 per year
- Perform a CSA and take an accelerated depreciation in the first five years, in which you could end up with more than $61,000 worth of depreciation in years 1–5. (If the analysis returns $200,000 worth of components that can be depreciated within the first five years, that's an additional $40,000 per year that can be depreciated.)
  - ($200,000 ÷ 5 years) + ($600,000 ÷ 27.5 years) = $61,000-plus for years 1–5. Then $21,000-plus for years 6–27.5.

Depreciation is the number-one way to legally reduce your personal tax liability by sheltering your income. It can also help you qualify for other tax credits and benefits. Why is that so important? Well, for every dollar you spend on taxes, it's a dollar you can't invest or put toward your wealth plan.

Even if you choose to not own the property outright, but rather invest in a passive real estate deal as an equity partner (also known as a syndication), depreciation can still benefit you as an investor.

Let's say you invest $100,000 in a passive real estate asset that is scheduled to throw off a 50 percent depreciation benefit in the first year, and let's say your effective tax rate is 37 percent. In the first year, you would get a $50,000 tax credit to use. How much would this save you? If we multiply that money by the tax rate you're paying, you'll realize that you end up saving $18,500, or 18.5 percent, for every $100,000 you've invested. As an investor, it gets even better—that asset might not even have generated $18,500, but you can use that depreciation to offset the income the asset is generating.

If this sounds too good to be true for you, it's probably because you still believe a few myths about taxes. I want to dispel one particular myth for you because I had these same thoughts when I started out, but discovering the truth freed me from that way of thinking—and it greatly helped me on my path to financial freedom.

Myth: If You Don't Pay Taxes, You're a Bad Person

This kind of thinking is deeply ingrained in us—somehow, lessening your tax burden makes us a little sleazy, or inherently evil. However, don't believe this myth. What has actually happened is that the *way* you pay taxes has changed. If you are investing in real estate or business, *your taxes are now at the asset level*, and if you lessen your personal tax burden legally, you're still paying local real estate taxes. You are also investing in local communities and perhaps hiring local contractors, vendors, and property managers to service the asset. In the end, you are positively impacting the local areas and employees where you invest.

I want you to add this information about taxes to your arsenal so that you can use it to navigate this potentially destructive horseman.

Step 2: Focus on Building Passive Income

There are two types of income: active and passive. If you want to enjoy lower taxes (and financial freedom), then you should intentionally focus on building passive income streams.

The IRS classifies employees or self-employed persons as active income earners, who get taxed at a higher rate. Business and investment income, on the other hand, is generally considered passive income and is usually taxed at a lower rate. The number of hours you spend on any given activity doesn't factor into the equation. Instead, it's purely based on what the IRS determines.

For example, if I have real estate notes that I spend no time managing, this is considered active income and is taxed at ordinary income rates. Let's say this income is $10,000 per year and is taxed at 22 percent. I will then owe $2,200 in taxes on that income. Netting $7,800 for almost no time involvement isn't too shabby, right?

However, if I pull in the same $10,000 on my rental properties and partnerships, I may be able to strategically use deductions to shelter the income and pay little to no tax on that income, simply because of the way the IRS classifies the income and allows me, as the business owner, to offset it.

Saving $2,200 on taxes may not be earth-shattering savings, but that is $2,200 more in my pocket to invest back into my business (in this case, real estate) and grow it!

The big idea is that those who earn income through their own business or earn from a company they invested in will pay the lowest taxes.

Step 3: Take Advantage of Lower Tax Brackets

Now it's time to partner with your tax strategist to look for ways to shift your income to lower tax brackets. You can do this by employing your dependents, if you have any.

Yes, I really mean to hire your kids if you have extra work that they can cover for you. It's legal.

If your child is under eighteen, they can work for you in your real estate business and earn up to their standard deduction (currently $13,850) before they have to pay taxes on income.

Just think: You could have your twelve-year-old file paperwork, clean the office, keep the books, and maybe manage your social media. In turn, at a young age they are learning work ethics, business skills, how to provide value to others, and how to invest. With what you pay them, they can use those funds to cover their expenses, save for college, start a Roth IRA, or invest alongside you. You still control the money; you just use their tax bracket.

I started this with my daughter when she was just four—she helped me file paperwork, and that's how she learned her ABCs. You can apply this same strategy to your own dependents.

However, you have to be careful. The IRS is fully aware of this tax loophole and is purposely looking for anyone mischievously taking advantage of it. Ensure that whatever your dependent is hired for that they are 1) capable of doing the job and 2) actually doing their job. You can't just place them on the payroll and not have them do anything. Otherwise, the IRS will call it out and disqualify the tax break.

Partner with your tax strategist to craft an accurate job description, determine a pay scale, and maintain proper documentation before hiring any dependents.

Step 4: Eliminate Income through Tax Credits

You might not know this, but you might qualify for a number of tax credits. Speak with your tax strategist for a personalized look into your situation.

Credits are a dollar-for-dollar reduction of income helping you reduce your tax liability. Some credits may apply to your personal tax situation; examples being the saver's credit, child tax credits, and investment credits.

Your business may also qualify for credits (research and development credits, employment credits, energy credits, water credits, tax abatements, and more). Credits are another way the IRS incentivizes behavior, so be sure to know what you qualify for.

Step 5: Defer Income to a Later Time

If you still want to reduce your taxable income after moving through the first four steps, then you should consider deferring your income. This means you can set aside part of your income to be taken in later years, like with a 401(k), IRA, or pension. This defers your tax to later years as well. This is also a helpful tactic to employ when you need to reduce your reported income just enough to be placed into a lower tax bracket.

If you are still working a W-2 job, it may be beneficial for you to fund your retirement accounts to maximize employer matches and pensions. That's still money that you may not want to lose.

If you choose to fund your retirement accounts, be sure to explore contributing to self-directed IRA accounts (SDIRAs) or other qualified retirement plans that are more in your control. With these types of accounts, you have more options to invest in alternative assets like real estate and various businesses while maximizing the tax code. For example, through an SDIRA, you can invest in:

- Real estate lending
- Fix-and-flips
- Buy and hold rentals
- Syndications and funds

Ask your tax strategist to create a model to see if funding these accounts will genuinely help your overall situation. It varies depending on where you live, your goals, and how much you make. Getting advice tailored to your specific situation is critical here.

We've talked about each of the four horsemen that can blow up your portfolio. Paying attention to them can save you thousands now, and even more in the future. However, you should still consider some other things.

Other Considerations for Your Portfolio

As you can probably tell, part of preparing your portfolio for the potential pitfalls of the four horsemen involves making the right choices and finding the right team of professionals. However, you may have a tax bomb sitting in your portfolio, especially if you contribute to retirement accounts like 401(k)s and traditional IRAs.

What am I talking about? It's this little-known thing called *provisional income*. Again, I'm not an accountant or tax strategist. This is a concept I learned from *The Power of Zero* by David McKnight.

When it's time for retirement, in order to sidestep the taxes arising from provisional income, you can take income from the following:

- **Roth IRA:** You already paid the taxes to put the money in there, so it grows tax-free and comes out tax-free.
- **Cash flow life insurance:** Similar to your Roth IRA, the money grows tax-free and comes out tax-free.
- **Tax-deferred IRAs:** As long as your required minimum distribution is below your standard deduction. At the time of writing, that's about $25,900 per year for a married couple. However, it's next to impossible to care for two people (let alone any children) on just that amount.

If you're putting all this money into your retirement accounts, and if you have more than $450,000 to $500,000 in your tax-deferred IRA (not Roth) by the time you retire, you'll end up paying taxes on any required minimum distributions you take at retirement above the standard deduction (right now it's $27,700 for a married couple). Withdrawing above the standard deduction also triggers provisional income rules and taxes on any social security income that you qualify for—jumping all the way up to 85 percent of your social security income in some cases.

Talk to a tax professional to ensure you have the correct setup for you so you don't end up paying provisional taxes. We will cover this strategy more in-depth in Chapter 12. For now, you want to do all you can to ensure you don't end up losing money in ways that can be avoided with proper planning.

═══ YOUR CHAPTER ACTION PLAN ═══

1. Take all tax deductions you are legally entitled to take.
2. Begin to shift how you earn your income—from active to passive.
3. Take advantage of lower tax brackets.
4. Qualify for and take tax credits.
5. Defer income to later years.

Real Stories of Money for Tomorrow
PRINCIPLES IN ACTION

Amanda Han, CPA, Keystone CPA

While there are countless strategies and approaches to building wealth, one often overlooked yet important aspect that can have a significant impact on wealth building is taxes. Or rather, tax savings.

Believe it or not, there is a close connection between tax savings and wealth building. With proper tax planning, we can unlock a multitude of opportunities to reduce our taxes. The taxes saved can then be redirected toward investments and, ultimately, the acceleration of wealth accumulation. This is the reason the wealthy always have a tax advisor on their team. Through smart tax planning, we can use the tools and tactics legally available. We can then be empowered to make informed decisions that not only optimize our tax position but also amplify our journey toward our financial goal. Whether it's taking a tax deduction on everyday things we are spending on our family or more advanced legacy planning, tax planning can be a powerful tool in our wealth building. Let's look at two stories here.

Leveraging Your Kid's Zero Percent Tax Bracket

When Christy decided to become a real estate investor, she had no idea just how much it would change her life. Not only has she been able to build up an impressive portfolio of rental properties, but she was also able to teach her teenage son about money and finances along the way.

One of the best things that Christy did while investing in real estate was hiring her son to help in her real estate. Instead of wasting his summer playing video games, Christy gave him tasks such as cleaning up rental properties, doing minor repairs, and taking care of administrative work. When he completed these tasks, she paid him for his time—and then got a tax deduction since it was business-related expenses.

Christy determined that the fair market value that she would pay someone to do these tasks was about $15 per hour. Based on the number of hours her son worked, Christy paid him a reasonable compensation of $3,600 for the summer. This became a tax deduction on her tax returns and saved her about $1,600 in taxes. Because her son did not have any other income, this summer's earnings were free from income taxes for him.

It was a win-win situation: Her son learned valuable lessons about money and responsibility while Christy saved money on taxes.

She also used this opportunity to teach her son about the importance of investing. She explained to him how saving the money he earned and reinvesting it in assets could be a good idea. He was able to see how real estate investments can pay off in the long run, how it's important to think ahead, and that patience and hard work can be rewarding. Her son saw firsthand, through his mother's example, the value of hard work and how successful investing can be.

Christy is a great example of how teaching kids about money and investing can be beneficial in more ways than one. Not only did she get to benefit from the tax deductions associated with hiring her son as a helper in her real estate business, but she also got to spend quality time with him and teach him lessons that would last a lifetime.

Legacy Planning

Mike purchased a property back in the 1980s for $100,000. Fast-forward to the present, and this property is now worth $1 million. Mike was getting up there in age and did not want to take care of the property anymore. Since he didn't need to live off of the cash flow from the property, he wanted to give the property to his daughter, Jen.

His first thought was simply to gift it to Jen. This seemed to be the easiest route to pass it to his only heir. At Jen's request, they made an appointment to meet with Mike's tax advisor to get his advice on whether this would be the right move. They were so glad they did—because the meeting completely changed their plan and saved them a ton in taxes.

Mike's tax advisor told them that gifting the property meant Jen's cost basis would be Dad's carry-over basis of $100,000. This means if Jen sold the property in the future, only $100,000 of that could potentially be tax-free. She would likely need to pay taxes on the rest.

However, if she inherited the property, she would receive a step-up basis for tax purposes. This means that when Jen inherits the property, her cost basis will be the fair market of the property at that point in time. To put it simply, this means that if Jen decided to sell the property after inheriting it, she would not have to pay capital gains taxes on any appreciation of the property during Dad's lifetime. Here is how the numbers would work:

Transfer via Gift	Transfer via Inheritance
$1,000,000 Sales Price	$1,000,000 Sales Price
– $100,000 Carry-Over Basis	– $1,000,000 Step-Up Basis
= $900,000 Taxable Gain	= $0 Taxable Gain
x 35% Tax Rate	x 35% Tax Rate
$315,000 Total Taxes Due	$0 Total Taxes Due

In this example, Mike waiting to pass this property to Jen until after his death via inheritance potentially saves Jen $315,000 in taxes versus if Mike had gifted it to her today.

When Mike and Jen discussed what they wanted to do with the property, it was a difficult decision. Ultimately, they both came to the realization that keeping the title of the property and allowing his daughter to inherit it was a win-win situation for both. Dad got to keep the property during his lifetime, and his daughter would benefit from not having to pay a very large capital gains tax when she eventually sold it.

This story serves as an example of how proper planning can protect valuable assets such as real estate from taxation while still allowing one generation to pass assets on to the next. It demonstrates how important it is for families to understand all available options when transferring assets between generations so they can make informed decisions about their financial future. And, just as importantly, understand why it is always a good idea to consult with a tax advisor on significant financial matters.

SECTION IV
Growing Wealth

CHAPTER 11

The Path to Becoming a Millionaire (and Beyond)

You don't need a complex plan to win at growing your wealth.

So far, we've touched on a little bit of everything that you need to know to create financial independence—how to build the foundation for wealth, how to create wealth, and what to do to keep the wealth you've created. It's not rocket science. Building wealth is about following sound principles and letting time do the work for you. It can be like watching paint dry, in a way—not super sexy or exciting in the moment. However, it gets exciting when you have your wealth and are able to travel and have adventures at your leisure!

But once you've mastered these principles, it's time to look toward the future: growing your wealth. Right now, it might seem a bit strange, maybe even a little far-fetched, to consider that you could be a millionaire in the near future—but it's possible for you, and this chapter is going to show you how.

The majority of millionaires are people just like you and me. Most of them didn't inherit fortunes or start hugely innovative companies. Instead, they followed simple, easily replicable principles that pushed them past the seven-figure mark—even starting with a regular salary from their day job.

So yes, it's possible for you.

As a matter of fact, it's inevitable once you start down this path. In this chapter, we're going to talk more about the path to growing your wealth and becoming a millionaire by breaking your growth plan into three manageable steps.

Step 1: Calculating Your Outcome Numbers for Your Financial Journey

As you know by now, I'm a HUGE proponent of planning. This is where I want you to put into practice everything you've learned so far about developing your mindset and the kind of life you want to create, and figure out your outcome numbers.

What do I mean by this? It's more than just discovering your *why*. This step is all about figuring out where you need to be financially to make your dream an actual reality.

Following all the work I've done with my clients through AshWealth.com, I've found that their goals fall into one of five buckets: financial security, financial vitality, financial independence, financial freedom, and absolute financial freedom.

Despite how similar they may sound, each of those goals has a different meaning. It's up to you to decide which of them align with your why. According to Tony Robbins in *MONEY: Master the Game*,[13] here are the definitions:

- **Financial Security:** Your assets generate enough cash flow to cover your rent or mortgage payments, grocery bills, utilities, household bills, transportation costs, and insurance premiums for at least a year.
- **Financial Vitality:** Your assets generate enough cash flow to cover everything in the Financial Security tier and at least half of your clothing bill, eating out, entertainment, and other small luxuries for at least a year.
- **Financial Independence:** Your assets generate enough cash flow to cover your current lifestyle without ever having to worry about working again.
- **Financial Freedom:** Your assets generate enough cash flow to cover your desired lifestyle without ever having to worry about working again.

---

13 Tony Robbins, *MONEY: Master the Game: 7 Simple Steps to Financial Freedom* (New York: Simon & Schuster: 2014).

- **Absolute Financial Freedom:** Your assets generate enough cash flow to allow you to do whatever you want, whenever you want, with whomever you want, as much as you want, without ever working again.

So how do you calculate your outcome numbers? If financial independence is your goal, make a list of what you spend monthly on your rent or mortgage payments, grocery bills, utilities, household bills, transportation costs, insurance premiums, clothing bills, eating out, entertainment, and small luxuries. Once you've got that desired monthly outcome number, multiply it by twelve and that's your annual outcome number for financial independence (i.e., your current lifestyle is covered by the cash flow of your investments for as long as you want).

When it comes to absolute financial freedom, however, you can allow yourself to dream as big as you dare—think of your current and future expenses, including things like owning multiple homes and cars, owning a private jet, or even an island. You can dream up extravagant quarterly vacations with your family and even include a line item for high-end jewelry or couture. The sky's the limit—literally. In this situation, your assets kick off cash flow to cover that level of lifestyle for as long as needed, moving you away from the lump-sum mentality of financial security or financial vitality.

Also, keep in mind you are on a wealth-building journey, so all are stops along that journey. Therefore, I want you to sit down and do this exercise and calculate your numbers for each financial journey milestone (security, vitality, independence, freedom, and absolute freedom), even if it makes you feel a little uncomfortable at first to dream this big.

I know that the first time I sat down and did this, the number that I ended up with as a goal seemed *huge.* I was worried about so many things, including whether or not I was deserving of that kind of success and how I would manage to pull it off.

This exercise is all about expanding your mind and allowing yourself to truly consider what's possible for you, and what you can achieve. It's only by getting honest and comfortable with these numbers that you'll actually be able to put yourself in a position to achieve them.

Another amazing thing that will happen for you, though, is you'll realize that so many things are *not as expensive as you thought.* For example, you may dream of having a boat one day, but what if you rented one now instead of buying it? Remember my mentor's sage advice: "Do you have to own it to have it?"

Step 2: Calculating Your Investment and Capital Numbers

Now that we have an idea of the kind of cash flow you'll need for each stop of your financial journey, it's time to move on to crunching numbers of *how* you'll get that cash flow. This will be determined by two calculations—your investment numbers and your capital numbers.

First, let's focus on what is needed to achieve financial independence. Your investment number is the amount of net cash flow an investment throws off. This number is entirely dependent on the investment, meaning that different investments have different investment numbers.

I'm very biased toward real estate investments. My single-family property's cash flow is between $275 and $300-plus per month per house *after all expenses and reserves have been set aside.* My passive investments throw off between $200 and $500 per month, depending on the investment. I even have some that throw off $1,000 or more per month. But the big factor is always for what kind of capital investment, risk exposure, and direct time involvement.

The net cash flow number, or investment number, is just one function of our equation to calculate our capital number, which looks something like this:

$$\left(\frac{\text{Monthly Required Cash}}{\text{Flow for Desired Outcome}} \div \frac{\text{Investment}}{\text{Number}} \right) \times \frac{\text{Cost of}}{\text{Investment}} = \frac{\text{Capital}}{\text{Required}}$$

So, let's say the number for your desired outcome that you identified in Step 1 of this exercise is $10,000 (i.e., your financial independence number). You want to invest in real estate, and each single-family home nets you $250 (investment number), and it costs $25,000 to purchase and get each one up and running (cost of investment number). If we plug those numbers into the equation, we get this:

$$(\$10,000 \div \$250) \times \$25,000 = \$1,000,000$$

We'll realize that we need to invest a total of $1,000,000 in capital (capital required) to get to a monthly cash flow of $10,000.

Now, that might sound like a lot, but remember these are all levers. If you increase your investment number to something like $275 or even $350, your capital-required number will decrease.

$$(\$10,000 \div \$275) \times \$25,000 = \$909,090$$

A second way to decrease your capital-required number is to bring down your cost of investment from $25,000 a door to $20,000 a door.

$$(\$10,000 \div \$250) \times \$20,000 = \$800,000$$

What if you could do both? That's the power of the third option, where you slightly raise your income as well as invest slightly less per door—that is, increasing your income and decreasing your expenses at the same time.

$$(\$10,000 \div \$275) \times \$20,000 = \$727,272$$

That's what is so great about this equation! You don't have to get a screaming deal for $0 down (don't get me wrong, that is nice). Even slight increases in your monthly income coupled with modest reductions in your capital required per asset can significantly decrease the capital needed to hit your goal.

However, you want to be realistic in your calculations. Just because you want $400 per door doesn't mean the market will give that to you right now. Maybe you have to take on an immense amount of risk to get that type of cash flow. It's all about balance. Keep in mind you will need to do some research on what is a reasonable cash flow for the asset you want to be in for the market you invest in.

Step 3: Three Assets You Can Invest In

Now that we've wrapped up the foundation of creating cash flow, it's time to talk about the top three assets you can invest in to start making your financial goals a reality. As I mentioned early on in this book, this doesn't constitute legal financial advice, and you really should speak to a qualified financial professional before deciding whether any of these suggestions would work well for your current situation.

Personally, I've invested in a plethora of things: stocks, bonds, mutual funds, bitcoin, real estate, businesses, ATMs, notes, and even collectibles. If you can name it, I've probably dabbled in it, here or there. However, even with all of these different kinds of investments, I always end up coming back to three core assets: business, real estate (my fave), and cash flow life insurance policies.

Why just these three assets? These are the only tax-favored assets entirely in your control. The IRS actually incentivizes people to invest in businesses and hold real estate by offering various tax breaks (see Chapter 10). A properly designed cash flow life insurance policy (see Chapter 6 for a definition) is an asset but technically isn't an investment; rather, it's a way to store money and possibly avoid paying taxes on the increased cash value later in life. (Note: I want to make it clear that Roth and other IRAs are not assets, and they are not in your control. The government actually controls them, and you are the beneficiary of the account, therefore they are not included in this list.)

If your goal is to reduce your tax position and reach your desired outcome number (i.e., your net income to support the lifestyle you chose for yourself in Step 1 of this exercise), then you should consider investing in business or real estate to achieve your investing goals. I love passive residential real estate (e.g., one-to-four-unit properties, small multi-family, mobile home parks), and *really* love it when I can combine real estate and a strong cash-flowing business (e.g., real estate syndications, self-storage, express car washes).

Where does that leave you? Take stock of the assets you already own and start thinking about how to maximize what you already have, as well as how to undertake new ventures. In the next chapter, I'll go more in-depth into investing principles to help guide your decision-making and assist you in making better investments.

═══ YOUR CHAPTER ACTION PLAN ═══

1. Calculate your outcome number for each milestone on your financial journey.
2. Calculate your capital requirements for your assumed investment number.
3. Understand the assets that have helped build tax-efficient wealth for the average investor.

Real Stories of Money for Tomorrow
PRINCIPLES IN ACTION

Kyle Wallitner, real estate investor, Issaquah, Washington

As a kid, I wasn't a very strong student, and I had a really hard time finding interest in anything to do with school. After graduating high school with a 1.8 GPA, I had a choice: move out of my parents' home or go to college. Since no big-time schools would have even considered taking me, I went into air traffic controller school and eventually got hired by the FAA.

While I was training at my air traffic control facility, I got the urge to buy my own house. At the time, I didn't want to "waste" money on rent. I knew houses appreciated in value, and my thought was I could recoup any home ownership costs through appreciation. In 2010 I bought my first home. It was a bigger house with extra space, allowing me to rent the basement to friends. This strategy would later become known as "house hacking."

So, there I was, twenty-five years old, excellent career, and I owned my own home. According to the traditional American narrative, everything was exceptional —or it should have been. But I wasn't happy. I knew there had to be something more than just waking up, going to work, mowing my little lawn on the weekends, and, if I was lucky, going on vacation two to three weeks a year to mask the fact that I was not fulfilled.

I felt awful, so I made a change.

Jumping into action, I enlisted the help of my longtime friend, and we devised a plan to buy a rental house. I was interested in the monthly cash flow, appreciation, and tax breaks that come with owning real estate. Plus, it was interesting to me. I leveraged my W-2 income to invest in something I enjoyed and was passionate about. So, I saved every cent I could to come up with my share of the down payment, and in 2012 we bought our first rental—a little three-bedroom, two-bath home in Puyallup, Washington, forty minutes south of Seattle.

On the weekends, my friend and I would work on the house, and eventually, we got it cleaned up and rented out. We were reaping the benefits of passive income, and a year later we bought our second rental house, then a third. We were weekend investor warriors: managing everything, including the rehab, alongside our normal W-2 jobs.

By 2015, the reality was sinking in. I wanted to scale faster, but continuing down the path I was on would take me a hundred years to get to where I wanted to be. Then it dawned on me: Why buy one rental when I can buy two or four with the same loan? I knew people bought larger properties and learned that the loan on a duplex, triplex, or fourplex was the same type of loan as the single-family home.

That next year, we bought a duplex and a fourplex. That's when everything changed. Up until that point, I thought I could only purchase ten homes with a conventional loan. I had no idea I could purchase ten fourplexes, meaning I could have forty doors! This was eye-opening. Viewing real estate as a vehicle and lending as the fuel propelled me and my portfolio forward. Building a team would be my next puzzle piece to solve.

When we purchased the fourplex (a huge undertaking), it marked the very first time we hired out property management. At first, I didn't think much of it. But then I realized how much time (and income) I was wasting doing my own rehabs at night on my duplex—five months, to be exact! That's when I decided enough was enough. We decided to use our property manager to complete the renovations on our new fourplex and take over the remaining renovations on the duplex. What had taken us five months to complete (or, in this case, not complete) took our property manager and their team only forty-five days to complete. Not only that, but it was also done correctly and efficiently.

After this experience, my entire outlook on real estate changed again. I made a complete 180 from doing everything myself to hiring a team. This mindset shift allowed me to scale rapidly over the next eighteen months.

My next deal was a twenty-unit apartment consisting of five separate fourplex buildings. Because I now had a team, I was putting in much less work than on any of the other properties I had bought in the past. Also, the twenty-unit was 2,000 miles away. I shifted from linear income to residual income by establishing a solid team, and now had the power and principles in place to purchase properties *anywhere* in the country.

You may be thinking that investing in real estate is something you can do on your own. But I can tell you that real estate is a team sport. Whether you have one single-family home or 10,000, you need a team. You see, it took me seven years to purchase my first ten doors, but because of my team, I have added another 125-plus doors in eighteen months. Not because I am anything exceptional, but because of my team. Take a look at anyone who has ever accomplished anything. They did not do it alone. Michael Jordan did not win six championships alone. Whitney Elkins-Hutten did not leave her W-2 to create AshWealth.com alone. Brandon Turner, David Greene—heck, the guy who owns Chick-fil-A—they all have a team.

Having a team is crucial, but I credit a lot of my success to one specific team member: the mentor. You can do all things if you believe you can. A mentor will help you with that. This person will open your eyes to what is possible if you let them. Be careful, though, because once you unlock that door, you'll see that anything really is possible, and there are infinite doors waiting for you on the other side. You just have to hold on tight and go through them.

CHAPTER 12

The Seven Principles of Conservative Investing

Wealth comes to those who learn to invest based on principles, not headlines.

Investing to grow your wealth might not be easy, but I do think it's simple. A bold statement. But my position comes from years of experience, as well as a deep understanding of what makes a good investor—being conservative. That's not what you expected, right?

After all, many of the investment gurus out there tout super returns and often promise people that they can become multimillionaires within just a few short years, or even months. That isn't my methodology. For every person who gets lucky and makes seven or eight figures in a few months, there are hundreds, probably even thousands, who end up derailed financially because they took on too much risk too soon.

Instead, we're going to be looking at the Seven Principles of Conservative Investing. These are tried-and-tested principles that have made many millionaires and billionaires and will make you one if you follow them closely. The best part about these principles? They have nothing to do with timing the market. They work in any market and allow you to build wealth in the midst of high inflation, market downturns, and even recessions.

The seven principles are separated into two categories: four tenets that help you hedge risk and performance, and three amplifiers that will accelerate your wealth building. We'll be taking a look at each.

Investing Principle #1: Capital Preservation

If you've ever done even a cursory search on information about investing, you've come across Warren Buffett. He's a prime example of conservative investing. When asked about his investing mantra, he boils it down to two rules:

> *Rule No. 1: Never lose money;*
> *Rule No. 2: Don't forget Rule No. 1.*
> — WARREN BUFFET, CEO OF BERKSHIRE HATHAWAY

As simple as it sounds, these two rules form the first tenet of a solid conservative investment strategy: preserving your capital. Regardless of the market cycle, it's imperative to invest in hard assets where your capital invested cannot go to zero. I love investing in real estate as much as I do because of this reason.

Additionally, this principle extends to investing in assets where you have control over the value of the asset. Any asset you invest in should have its value based on net operating income or expected gross income, not on market changes. Lastly, choose an asset that is well capitalized with capital expenditure and operational reserves to mitigate loss and to prevent the need to sell in a down market unnecessarily. The whole idea of building a core portfolio of assets that preserves capital is so you do not get knocked out of the investing game!

Investing Principle #2: Cash Flow

The second tenet of conservative investing is to choose assets that have multiple streams of income, with cash flow starting on *day one* of owning the asset, instead of waiting for the cash flow to kick in months later. You want *immediate* cash flow, which is only possible if the asset has an element of stability in today's market. Even if the cash flow is low—say, 3 percent to 4 percent cash-on-cash return—you want to have a solid business plan to grow the cash flow over your holding period.

In the case of real estate, you can protect your cash flow by researching several rental comps in the area that are higher than the property you're about to invest in, so you can be competitive in the market should you need to adjust rents. This principle also goes back a little to the first tenet of capital preservation—you want to ensure that the asset is well capitalized with several months of operational reserves from day one to mitigate any sort of loss and to protect the current cash flow on the asset.

Investing Principle #3: Equity Growth

In the investing world, you see two kinds of equity growth: natural market growth and forced equity growth. In an ideal situation, you want to stack the investing cards in your favor and choose assets that take advantage of *both* kinds of growth.

To tap into natural market growth potential with an asset, you need to choose investments in areas of your country where the population is growing, jobs are growing, incomes are increasing, more diverse jobs are being created, and poverty and crime are decreasing. You have no control over these things, so this requires a bit of research. You'd also do well to invest in markets with favorable business tax structures to keep one of your largest expenses down.

In the case of forced equity growth, you'll need to be on the lookout for assets where you can make targeted investments that can increase the income it throws off, decrease the expenses associated with it, or contribute additional streams of income into the asset. The real power is when you're able to meet all three of these requirements at the same time.

Investing Principle #4: Tax Benefits

The four tenets of conservative investing revolve around choosing assets that have tax benefits associated with them. The IRS incentivizes investing in certain assets to solve certain problems, and you can benefit from this.

When you invest in real estate, you can create paper losses through depreciation, including accelerated depreciation and bonus depreciation. These losses can help shelter the income your asset generates from taxation. Additionally, you can benefit from the 1031 exchange when you invest in real estate, which gives you the ability to defer the tax on capital gains and avoid depreciation recapture. The tax benefits of real estate are one of the most powerful ways to build wealth because you get to maximize the time value of money and take what you would have paid in taxes and invest it *today* to amplify your wealth build.

Once you adhere to these four tenets of conservative investing, you'll be able to evaluate your investments for their long-term value as well as hedge risks, making it possible for you to experience growth even in the midst of an economic downturn. But once you've got these tenets down, what can you do to amplify your investments? Let's take a look.

Investing Principle #5: Inflation Hedge

The first investment amplifier is an inflation hedge. Most investors just look at the loan on the property as the best asset for inflation, since you are locking in one of your largest expenses (the debt) and letting inflation (the decreased purchasing power of the currency) erode the debt over time. However, using real estate as an example, once you invest in a property, you can periodically increase your income by periodically passing through expense increases to the end customer. The reason this works is because, as the investor, you get to manipulate the income and expenses on the asset.

In the case of multifamily properties, you have an opportunity to increase your income annually when it's time to renew the leases of your tenants—for example, increasing rents from $50 to $100 a month per unit renewed. For self-storage properties, you have an opportunity to increase your income monthly. For express car washes or hotels, it's possible to increase your income daily. With an inflation hedge, you can respond to the market to protect your purchasing power as needed—making this amplifier one of the most powerful aspects of conservative investing.

Investing Principle #6: Leverage

So far, I've talked about leverage a lot in this book, so it's no surprise I consider it to be a huge amplifier of wealth. In this context, it means understanding how to safely arbitrage the interest rate environment and grow your wealth. When the interest rates are on the rise, it creates a cycle where fixed-rate debt covering the term of the hold on any project is KING, and short-term floating-rate debt should be used with immense caution.

What does that mean for you? For most everyday millionaires, fixed-rate debt should always be the preference because you are able to lock in one of your largest expenses for a longer period of time: the cost of the debt. This will help you mitigate any increased debt costs should interest rates increase, as they did most recently in 2022 and 2023.

If purchasing an asset with fixed-rate debt isn't an option and you need to use floating-rate debt, it's best to ensure that the debt has a rate cap (meaning you have purchased an insurance policy that would cap the amount of interest you would pay, which reduces your risk for inflated interest rates). Additionally, ensure the project has been underwritten at the rate cap for the duration of the hold. While the cost of your debt might increase should interest rates start to climb, you will have locked in a max cost of that debt while being able to take advantage of any short-term interest rate drops. In 2022 and 2023, many operators and investors struggled to hold onto their assets and were caught off guard by how quickly their debt costs rose as interest rates skyrocketed. Unfortunately, not everyone was able to hold onto these assets, and many had to sell quickly for a loss to avoid losing the asset to bankruptcy.

In addition, since floating-rate debt is generally used for short-term projects (say, one to three years), you should ensure the operator has also negotiated periodic loan extensions to the debt term upfront to cover the hold period, and has multiple avenues built into the business plan for a successful exit should the market go sideways or south. For me, this means if the project had an anticipated timeline of three years, the floating-rate debt should be at least three years long and have another two one-year extensions negotiated in, should the project take longer for whatever reason.

Investing Principle #7: Invest with Experts

If there's one amplifier I want you to adopt from this list—even if you don't really utilize the others—it's this one. Choosing to invest with what you know, like, and trust is, without a doubt, the most important conservative investing pillar in *any* asset. If you are the operator, then you have to take on being the expert. Those who professionally manage traditional 401(k) stock bonds and mutual funds have been trained to look for yield, making them drawn to investments with high returns, but the success of any deal hinges more on the operator's execution. So it's no wonder many new investors get into hot water. This is especially true in real estate.

I've come to realize I just can't be the expert in every aspect of real estate. That's why it's so important to invest in a team with:

- Knowledge of the investment strategy.
- A track record of positive performance.
- The ability to secure credit and lending for high-quality assets.
- The ability to reliably pool capital to close and manage the asset.
- A professional team to source, acquire, operate, and reposition any deal in their portfolio on your behalf.

When you find an investment expert like that, you can not only feel confident they will preserve your initial investment and execute their business plan, but they will also get you your time back—your most valuable, nonrenewable resource. While we can't cover all aspects of how to find great operational experts, I teach how to do this at AshWealth.com.

These seven investing principles have helped me grow my wealth to where it is today, and have helped make millionaires over the decades. Before I go into any investment, I grade each asset in my portfolio for these seven pillars to ensure I have stacked as many wealth principles in my favor as possible—be it a single-family rental property or larger commercial building, or when I eventually started investing in private equity real estate.

Alternative Investment Continuum

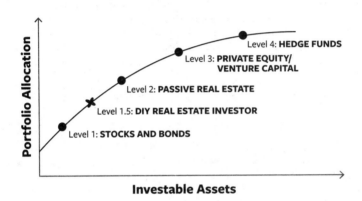

Even though we can't be sure what the future will hold as far as investments and recessions go, you can be sure these principles will help you to weather any "storm" that may come. Investors who followed these principles made money through all twelve modern recessions, and they were *successful* even when the market wasn't as favorable.

═══ YOUR CHAPTER ACTION PLAN ═══

1. Grade each of your current assets according to the Seven Principles of Conservative Investing.
2. Consider repositioning any capital into an asset that adheres to all Seven Principles of Conservative Investing.
3. Grade every new investment you are considering making according to the Seven Principles of Conservative Investing prior to making your investment decision.

Real Stories of Money for Tomorrow
PRINCIPLES IN ACTION

Todd Gabianelli, passive real estate investor, Arlington Heights, Illinois

My investing journey beyond the stock market started when I was looking for ways to replace my wife's income as we were starting to plan for a family. I was in a high-paying W-2 sales position and wanted to find investment opportunities that offered spendable cash flow beyond what I could find in an index fund or 401(k) investment. I had read Robert Kiyosaki's book *Rich Dad, Poor Dad* several times, and the philosophy of using other people's money to purchase assets that appreciated and put money in my pocket really resonated with me.

After reading the book, my first passive-income goal was to create enough income for my wife to be able to leave her elementary school teaching job to stay at home with our new daughter. I settled on buying turnkey single-family rentals in landlord-friendly states, as this approach seemed to be the most "passive" and easiest for me to outsource to property management. My strategy was to purchase two properties per year using 80 percent leverage and use the cash flow from those properties to replace my wife's income. After several years, I purchased ten single-family properties and realized that the cash flow was significantly less than I had expected. Dealing with the property managers took more time than I would have liked, and the costs of maintenance, repairs, and tenant turnovers ate away much of the returns.

It was at this same time that I had hit the Fannie Mae loan limit of ten loans and realized I didn't have the bandwidth or interest in purchasing more properties, but really wanted to continue investing in real estate. I mentioned this challenge to a business coach and mentor who I was working with at the time. He suggested that, since I was now an accredited investor, I should look into real estate syndications and private equity investments. This option seemed to offer exactly what I was looking for: strong risk-adjusted returns, and the ability to invest alongside experienced operators across multiple types of commercial real estate spread out in different geographic areas across the country. I quickly leveraged his experience and connections to shortcut my path into investing as a limited partner and got introduced to three general partners/operators in multifamily apartment buildings who were raising money for new deals.

What attracted me to these opportunities was the fact that once I completed my due diligence on the operator, the market, and the actual property, I simply had to wire my funds and then wait for the distributions to hit. After that first distribution hit my bank account, there was no looking back. I had found an investing strategy that provided greater returns than I was getting in single-family rentals, significantly less time, and more consistent monthly cash flow than managing my own rental properties.

Additionally, as my net worth continued to grow, this strategy allowed me to limit my liability to just the amount of my initial investment. No calls from property managers, no calls at midnight from tenants—just a monthly distribution check and a report from the operator on the financials for that month. True mailbox money.

Since my first syndication investment as an LP, I have invested in close to twenty different syndications and real estate private equity funds across five different asset classes (multifamily, mobile home communities, RV parks, self-storage, and car washes). Further, I have diversified my invested capital across multiple geographic areas and seven different operators, further minimizing my capital exposure to any one single asset class, operator, or geographic area. Today, I've repositioned most of my equity into these types of investments, which yield a six-figure annual income for my family—covering all of our living expenses and putting us on the path of complete "lifestyle" freedom.

So how could someone replicate my journey? The first part of my investing journey was using the leverage of the banks to get started buying properties when I had less money. This move allowed me to own physical assets and not be at the mercy of the day-to-day swings of the stock market. As my portfolio grew, I began to leverage operators, syndicators, and due diligence partners to find new investment opportunities, allowing me to spend more time with my family. I joined a real estate investor–focused mastermind that not only provides access to deal flow that I would otherwise never see, but also offers opportunities for networking and building relationships with new and experienced operators. Being a part of this group of like-minded investors provides additional due diligence on investment opportunities beyond what my skills and time allow for. Not every deal is a home run—in fact, most of mine have been singles and doubles—but I enjoy having a trusted personal relationship with the general partners (GPs)/operators now on most of the deals that I invest in.

There are many paths to financial freedom and job optionality; the key is finding the one that works for you. For me, buying single-family rentals until I had achieved accredited investor status gave me the knowledge and experience to learn that I did not want to focus full-time on real estate investing. My career is my focus, as it provides a high income and I still enjoy it. Until this job is no longer fulfilling to me, I plan to continue investing as an LP and watch the monthly distributions continue to grow.

=== CHAPTER 13 ===

Investing Concepts to Master

*If investing were easy,
everyone would be successful at it.*

With all those investing principles in mind, let's take a deep dive into the *application* of what we've just learned. Knowing all the principles doesn't automatically mean you'll be great at choosing the best investment for your goals.

Fortunately, there's a formula for that—and that's what we'll be discussing right now.

The Simple Math Equation to Help You Figure Out Your Asset Performance

This whole framework revolves around answering an important question: Does your equity work hard for you, or are you working hard for your equity? By figuring this out, you'll have a clear picture of which investments you should keep and which ones you need to reposition or get rid of altogether.

The logic behind figuring out your asset performance is rooted in a math equation I like to call the Investment Index.[14] Essentially, you find this index by taking your monthly cash flow and dividing it by

---

14 Chris Miles, Money Ripples.

your initial investment. Similar to the Cash Flow Index we discussed in Chapter 7, this number is going to serve as your North Star when it comes to determining the health of your investments.

Initial Investment ÷ Monthly Cash Flow = Investment Index

After doing the calculation, you want to have a number that's less than 75. Any investment with an Investment Index lower than 75, you want to keep. If any of your other investments come up short and end up above that number, you can reposition your portfolio by selling, refinancing, or even raising rents (if it's a real estate or business investment you control).

Keep in mind this isn't a one-and-done exercise. You should update your Investment Index annually to determine how your assets are performing.

Here is an example from my portfolio. In 2020, we purchased a two-unit property, in a mountain town in Colorado, where we hope to retire to in a few years. We purchased the property for $610,000, put $124,224 down, and were cash-flowing $1,200 a month with both units rented. According to the formula above, this wasn't a good investment since the index was 104.

$124,224 down payment ÷ $1,200 monthly cash flow = 104

However, we knew the market well and knew that rents were low and would continue to increase significantly. Over the next two years we made some key upgrades—including expanding storage on the property—so we could grow our rents. Today, the property cash-flows $1,900 a month with both units rented, and the new index is 65. Now we are below the 75 Investment Index threshold and this property makes sense to keep.

$124,224 down payment ÷ $1,900 monthly cash flow = 65

What is more enlightening is this formula allows you to quickly compare and contrast the performance of real estate, notes, stock market portfolio, and any bank products in your portfolio. If we apply this formula to a bank CD that I have set aside for emergency expenses (currently earning 5 percent annualized cash flow), you can see the Investment Index on this CD is 240. Not good.

$30,000 CD investment ÷ $125 monthly cash flow = 240

Alternatively, I have a duplex in which I invested $30,000 as the down payment, and it earns $575 a month net cash flow. The Investment Index is 52 for this investment—a huge difference from 240 with my bank CD!

$30,000 down payment ÷ $575 monthly cash flow = 52

This exercise is one of my favorites. Why? Because it takes away all the emotions and sentimental value and drills straight down to the most important part of any investment decision: Is my equity working hard enough to help me reach my investing goals?

If it is, great. But if it isn't, you have to come up with a plan. If you want to keep the asset, restructuring it is a must. However, you also need to figure out why you're holding it even though it isn't doing well. This evaluation is an ongoing process, one you'll need to initially do quarterly to ensure that you have a good handle on your asset performance.

The Opportunity Cost of Not Investing in Real Estate

I'm a staunch believer that investing in real estate is one of the most predictable ways to create generational wealth—to move from working for your money to having your money work for you. But I'm also aware that many people might not exactly be *excited* about the idea of real estate, especially in a market riddled with inflation and the possibility of us heading back into a recession at the time of this writing.

However, there *is* an opportunity cost when it comes to not investing in real estate. Even with all the possible negatives, once you head back to the fundamentals and use them to make an educated decision with your money based on tried-and-true principles and understanding the math, you'll find there's real wealth to be created in *any* real estate market. You could be missing out on a real opportunity by choosing not to invest when times seem uncertain.

That's why in this section I want to help you identify the opportunity costs you're incurring by staying on the sidelines, or even by choosing to invest in another asset instead of real estate.

When I mention opportunity cost, I'm talking about the value or benefit you give up by engaging in one activity relative to another. Basically, the opportunity cost is the math behind what you're giving up when you make a different decision.

Let's say we're looking at two different investment options. Option 1 has a 10 percent return, while Option 2, the one that you're currently investing in, has a 2 percent return. If you choose to stay with Option 2, then your opportunity cost would be:

$$10\% - 2\% = 8\%$$

Now, with that 8 percent calculation, you might be surprised and think, "Wow, I'm giving up 8 percent return on my money." However, the math gets more interesting when you start introducing real numbers. Let's say you have $100,000 invested in Option 2 that's only yielding you 2 percent—a vehicle like a savings account, for example.

Now, what are you giving up relative to investing in Option 1? Put in real numbers, that's $8,000 per year.

$$\$100,000 \times 8\% = \$8,000$$

However, it's even more than that because you are losing out on $8,000 each year you don't make a different choice, and all the potential compounded growth over time. Let's take a deeper dive into the math.

Let's say we took just *one year* of that $8,000 loss and invested it the following year in Option 1, which yields 10 percent per year for around thirty years. That's almost $80,500 you gave up by choosing for just *one year* to invest in an asset that could yield you 10 percent instead of 2 percent.

$$\frac{\$8,000 \text{ invested at } 10\% \text{ compounded}}{\text{annually for 30 years}} = \$80,500$$

Mind-blowing, right? Now think about how much that could become if you were adding $8,000 to that 10 percent investment *every* year. It would be $985,000 over thirty years!

Believe it or not, this example is actually pretty forgiving in today's investment climate. In today's environment, the percentage discrepancy we could be looking at between two investment options would be something more like 14 percent and 70 percent. This is generally the kind of opportunity cost difference between the assets that people are choosing, which ends up hurting them in the long run.

Of course, being able to identify the opportunity cost of investments all boils down to having the right way of evaluating opportunities, which is something we discussed in Chapter 9 on the Seven Principles of Conservative Investing. But now, let's look at them through a different lens: real estate.

Real Estate and Capital Preservation

This principle, pioneered by Warren Buffett, is all about ensuring you're preserving your money and not losing it. But how can you be sure? By keeping it in a bank, your money will lose value. Even if we weren't in this high-inflation environment, you would be losing 2 percent to 3 percent of the value of your money thanks to the Fed raising interest rates.

What else can you invest in? You can start looking at stocks, bonds, mutual funds, or even cryptocurrency. Or you can look into secured hard assets—assets where the value is determined by the operating income they bring in or the expected gross income they are bringing in. From my personal experience—and the experience of billionaires like Warren Buffett, Dale Carnegie, and the Rothschild family—secured hard assets are always the way to go.

You want to invest in an asset that might not be the top dog in the area. It could be an undervalued business, or an undervalued piece of real estate relative to other properties in the area. That gives you the chance to grow, as well as make sure you have enough reserves to maintain the asset so you don't have to sell if the market gets challenging.

This principle is the first way that investing in real estate gives you the chance to make *more* money than you would if you invested in other assets like stocks, bonds, and cryptocurrency.

Real Estate and Cash Flow

This second principle comes directly from my good friend Ryan Lee of Cashflow Tactics,[15] and is best illustrated through an example.

Ryan tells the story of two tree planters. One goes out and plants beautiful loblolly pine trees because he wants to make his money through paper. The other plants apple trees. The apple tree might not be worth as much as a loblolly pine that's going to become paper in thirty years, but he'll be able to start harvesting apples seasonally within six to eight years, *every single year.*

---

15 Ryan Lee, "Our Story," Cashflow Tactics, Accessed July 4, 2023, https:// cashflowtactics. com/our-story/.

Unlike the planter who has to wait a long time to get a lump sum payment from his pine tree, the planter who chose an apple tree will be able to make money earlier and faster, and he doesn't have to cut down his apple tree. The point?

You want to look for assets that have great cash flow potential, ideally in a situation where you don't even have to wait very long for your asset to start cash-flowing. Usually, we want cash flow from *day one*, not six to eight years later, as with an apple tree. Additionally, you want to make sure that your expenses are pretty low relative to your cash flow.

Let's say that the unit or the building you bought is bringing in $100,000 per month. That's pretty high, right? But let's say that your expenses end up being $95,000 per month to keep that investment afloat. All of a sudden, it doesn't look as appealing, does it? When it comes to real estate, we want our expenses to be pretty low so that we have a healthy margin not only to replenish our operational reserves, but also a way to make a profit for ourselves.

Real Estate and Equity Growth

Everyone is drawn to investments that appreciate well. For the majority of investments, the market determines the appreciation or depreciation of your investment. In the ideal situation, you don't want to rely on the market for your appreciation and depreciation of an asset. Instead, you want to be able to *control* the appreciation of your assets. Assets like bitcoin and gold fall into this category. I have a little of each in my portfolio, but I can't control their appreciation, so investing in them isn't a major part of my wealth-building strategy. It shouldn't be part of yours either.

Instead, I use real estate as the major wealth-building vehicle in my portfolio. I can stack my investing cards in my favor by being in a market with high growth, giving me room to progress and grow. I can also invest in assets that allow me to increase my income and decrease expenses, as well as assets that contribute additional streams of income.

By increasing the net operating income of an asset, you can force the appreciation of an asset. This is just the way commercial real estate values are determined.

$$\text{Net Operating Income} \div \text{Cap Rate} = \text{Commercial Real Estate Asset Value}$$

The equation above does have one variable we need to define, and that is the market cap rate. The cap rate is the most popular measure through which real estate investments are assessed for their profitability and return potential. The cap rate simply represents the yield of a property over a one-year time horizon, assuming the property is purchased with cash and not with a loan.

While you can't necessarily control the cap rate for your asset in your market, once you're increasing the net operating income of your asset, even if the cap rate rises as well, it is very possible you are still increasing the value of the asset. Let's take a look.

Let's say you purchase an eight-unit multifamily building that is generating $60,000 annually in net operating income, and the current market cap rate is 5 percent. The value of the asset would be $1,200,000.

$$\$60,000 \div 5\% = \$1,200,000$$

Let's say over the next year, you are able to modestly raise rents $75 a door per month and slightly decrease expenses by $25 a door per month, for a net operating income increase of $100 a door per month—or $9,600 annually. If the market cap rate stays the same at 5 percent, the new value of your building is $1,392,00—a $192,000 increase in just one year.

$$\$69,600 \div 5\% = \$1,392,000$$

But what if the market is getting hotter and the cap rate starts dropping? After one year, the new cap rate in the market is 4.9 percent. The new value of the building would be $1,420,408—a $28,408 increase in just one year.

$$\$69,600 \div 4.9\% = \$1,420,408$$

However, if the local real estate market is getting worse (e.g., the market cap rate starts increasing), and the new cap rate in the market is 5.2 percent, then the new value of your building would be $1,388,461.

$$\$69,600 \div 5.2\% = \$1,338,461$$

Because you control the operations of the asset, making slight changes to income and expenses that grow the overall net operating income of the asset can still result in significant commercial real estate value increases, even in a softening market.

In the end, as a real estate investor, purchasing good assets in good markets that are valued based on net operating income could enable you to make money in a market that may be going up, going down, or slipping sideways.

Real Estate and Tax Benefits

You could be missing out on *many* tax advantages of investing in real estate, especially buy and hold real estate.

Recall Chapter 10: Paying taxes is eroding your chance to accelerate your wealth growth. And the tax benefits of real estate, in the form of depreciation, is one of the largest and most accessible tax shelters out there.

Also remember, the IRS tax code is essentially a treasure map, and the IRS wants you to take depreciation, be it straight-line or accelerated depreciation (they will penalize you if you *don't* take it). Depreciation is the number-one way to legally reduce your personal tax liability by sheltering your income and qualifying for other tax credits and benefits. For every dollar you save on taxes, it's a dollar you can invest or put toward your wealth plan.

You can also defer capital gains that essentially push your tax bill down the road—meaning if you die with your assets in your name or your company's name and you haven't gifted them to any heirs, that tax bill may essentially evaporate through current IRS step-up in basis rules.

These are some of the reasons why I'm so adamant about investing in real estate. You're losing out on so much by not considering this as a viable option for creating generational wealth.

Real Estate and Inflation Hedging

Real estate is one of the best—if not *the* best—inflation hedges in the world of investment. Why? Because you have the ability to use fixed-rate debt to lock in one of your largest expenses now and let the devaluation of the current inflation erode the debt for you. At the same time, you have the ability to raise the income on the asset in response to market demands and pass any fixed or variable expense increases you have through it as well.

I can renegotiate a multifamily contract annually, my self-storage contracts monthly, and my short-term rental prices nightly. This gives me insane leverage to protect my investments from inflation, creating a hedge that is practically unheard of in other kinds of investments.

Real Estate and Leverage

The crazy thing about real estate is that it can depreciate AND appreciate (increase in value) at the same time. Although appreciation is not a guarantee—rather the icing on the cake—the average home appreciation in the U.S. has been 4.3 percent annually since 1991, and 7.7 percent annually since 2012.[16] But through smart use of leverage (i.e., a loan), you can amplify this return and build your wealth faster.

Let's say you purchase a $100,000 property and the market appreciation in your area is 6 percent annually. Therefore, after you hold your $100,000 property for one year, the value increases to $106,000. If you purchased this home all in cash, your appreciation return would only be $6,000.

$$\frac{\$6{,}000}{\text{(market appreciation)}} \div \frac{\$100{,}000}{\text{(capital invested)}} = \frac{6\%}{\text{(appreciation return)}}$$

However, you decided to take a bank loan for $80,000 and only put down $20,000 for the home. Now your return from appreciation is magnified because you earn $6,000 on your investment of $20,000—therefore your leveraged return from appreciation is actually 30 percent, not 6 percent.

$$\frac{\$6{,}000}{\text{(market appreciation)}} \div \frac{\$20{,}000}{\text{(capital invested)}} = \frac{30\%}{\text{(levered appreciation return)}}$$

Leverage can also amplify the cash-on-cash return of your asset—the cash income earned on the cash you have invested in the asset.

Let's say you rent the $100,000 home you own all in cash for $1,100 a month. At the end of the month, you clear $800 after all expenses are paid (property taxes, insurance, and reserves). In this case, your cash-on-cash return would be 9.6 percent.

$$(\$800 \times 12 \text{ months}) \div \$100{,}000 = 9.6\%$$

Now let's say you decide to take that same bank loan for $80,000 at 6 percent and only put down $20,000 for the home. At the end of the month, you clear $221 after all expenses are paid (loan principal, mortgage interest, taxes, insurance, and reserves). In this case, your cash-on-cash return would be 13.3 percent.

$$(\$221 \times 12 \text{ months}) \div \$20{,}000 = 13.3\%$$

---

16 https://www.creditkarma.com/home-loans/i/average-home-value-increase-per-year#:~:text=Since%201991%2C%20the%20average%20annual,significantly%20from%20state%20to%20state.

One of the advantages of using leverage is you can now buy five homes that cash flow $221, each with only a $20,000 down payment per home, instead of just one home. This allows you to spread out your equity across multiple homes. Also, the leverage amplifies your cash, since it would now be $1,105 (5 x $221) instead of $800.

The whole point of this section is to help you understand how to use leverage (i.e., lending) *smartly* to create generational wealth. The name of the game when it comes to leverage is we want to be able to use debt to safely arbitrage the interest rate environment. Simply, we want the cash flow from the asset to more than pay for the debts and expenses associated with the hold of the asset. While leverage used incorrectly can wreak havoc on your wealth (as we saw in Chapter 3), leverage used properly can spring-load your financial situation.

Some Rules to Remember
How can you use leverage smartly? I have a few rules when I'm looking for assets.

- I choose a fixed interest rate, if possible, or if there's a floating rate, I want it to be capped, limiting my lending risk.
- For single-family properties or small multifamily units (under four units), fixed debt terms are common. But for bigger assets, you'll probably only be able to get a fixed term for the first five or ten years.

There are a few other things you want to look out for when you're investing in assets that have a loan associated with them, like the following:

- Secure debt for at least the term of the business plan, if not longer, to give you some wiggle room for a reposition or an exit. For example, if you are purchasing a property and plan to hold it for five years before selling, placing a five-year loan on the property would be just enough time to complete your business plan. A seven-year loan would give you a couple of years of breathing room should the market change.
- You want the ability to negotiate extensions on your loan or refinance terms. For example, if your business plan calls for an extensive rehab over a three-year hold, you can negotiate into your purchase term sheet the ability to extend the current debt terms for one or two years for a small fee. That way you aren't pressured to complete the rehab, stabilize your project, and then sell or refinance in a less than ideal market.

- You want debt that has low or no lockout periods or prepayment penalties. This gives you the ultimate flexibility to sell earlier than your desired hold timeline and not be penalized with a high fee or not be able to sell at all due to a lockout period.
- Lastly, you will also want debt that is fixed-rate debt—meaning the interest rate doesn't change—or floating-rate debt with an interest rate cap. Many investors purchased property with floating-rate debt in 2019–2022, thinking that the Federal Reserve wouldn't possibly move interest rates that quickly. That changed fast in 2022, when the Federal Reserve hiked the federal funds rate from 2.5 percent to over 4.5 percent in six months (in Q4 2023, the federal funds rate is 5.5 percent and climbing). This type of rapid interest rate movement caused many assets to go from positive cash flow to negative cash flow in a very short time period. Those investors who didn't have a cap on how high their interest rate could go were in a serious pickle by January 2023, with many losing their assets to the bank.

By taking these four things into consideration, you'll be able to create massive leverage while investing in real estate—which is something that you'll be hard-pressed to find in other kinds of investments.

Real Estate and Opportunity Cost

Investing in real estate allows you to hedge against inflation and preserve your capital since you're investing in growth markets with cash flow. You can pull the equity lever whenever you want, making it possible for you to increase income and decrease expenses, as well as add extra income streams if you need to—you can annually increase your rent. Investing in real estate also gives you some amazing tax advantages that are only available to real estate investors.

If you're looking to create generational wealth, investing in real estate is one of the best investments you can make. You might find yourself losing wealth rapidly or taking outsize risks for returns if you choose not to add real estate to your portfolio. At the end of the day, the opportunity cost of not investing in real estate allows you to make asymmetric risk-mitigated returns built on multiple wealth principles.

The Power of the Zero Percent Tax Bracket

This is one of my favorite topics: the power of getting to the point where you pay zero percent taxes. I learned this from David McKnight in his book *The Power of Zero*.[17]

You might not actually get to zero, but it's all about how close you get—like maybe 10 percent or 15 percent overall. It's kind of like the saying that if you shoot for the moon, you'll land in the stars, and that's still a pretty great place to be.

Before we go any further, I want to be explicit: This is not tax evasion. In fact, we're following a principle based on a Supreme Court decision set forth in 1935 by Judge Learned Hand. I mentioned it in Chapter 10, and here it is again:

"Anyone may arrange his affairs so that his taxes shall be as low as possible; he is not bound to choose that pattern which best pays the treasury. There is not even a patriotic duty to increase one's taxes." [18]

So what did Judge Hand mean? In short, you aren't given gold stars for paying more taxes. In fact, you should do what you can to arrange your affairs and money to reduce your tax bill as much as you can. Doing so frees up more cash to put toward your investing goals and value-based spending, as well as contribute more to your charities of choice.

Recall Chapter 4 on linear income versus residual passive income—how you earn your income. Employees pay the most taxes since they are not taking any business risks, and get very few ways to reduce their tax bill. On the opposite end of the spectrum, the investor is taking risks in the world, investing in someone else's business, where jobs are created in the economy and essential goods and services are provided. This means for business owners and investors that all the taxes they incur are deductible, meaning they'll end up with an overall lower tax rate.

In addition to this, we get taxed in different income categories, or "buckets," as I like to call them. When our income comes in, we can choose which of these buckets to put our income into, and this will end up influencing the amount of taxes we pay. These buckets are broken down into three different kinds: taxable, tax-deferred, and tax-free.

---

17 David McKnight, *The Power of Zero: How to Get to the 0% Tax Brack and Transform Your Retirement* (revised and updated) (New York: Crown, 2018).

18 Gamburg, "How to Legally Maximize."

Taxable

This is when you move your income into your bank account or a brokerage account and it just sits as cash or savings. When you have your money sitting in a cash or savings account, you are actually repeatedly taxed on this money in the form of ordinary income tax on that interest earned. This tax will compound the larger the account grows.

Tax-Deferred

If you choose to invest your income in a traditional IRA vehicle, that money goes in tax-free and grows tax-free, and you don't have to pay the taxes until withdrawal at the end. (However, this might not be the benefit we think it is, as I, and many experts, believe that tax rates will possibly go up, not down, in the future.)

Tax-Free

This bucket is the one we're most interested in, and it's where you want to be. You take your income and, though you've already paid taxes on it, you put it in a position where it's able to grow tax-free. This bucket includes things like a Roth IRA where you've already paid the taxes upfront, so it grows tax-free and comes out tax-free; or when you convert your IRA to Roth so you pay the taxes on it and then it grows tax-free and comes out tax-free. While those two options are well and good, the problem with them is that they are under government control. You don't have complete control over the funds as they are in a "for-benefit" account you can't touch, and the government can change the rules pretty much at any time.

However, two other options in the tax-free bucket that give you greater control over your own money are cash flow life insurance and real estate. Also known as infinite banking, cash flow life insurance is a specialized policy that you won't be able to get by just going to your agent down the street. This policy helps you to maximize the amount of cash flow you make from the policy. We don't really care about the death benefit here; instead, you carry just enough death benefit for however much you want to save there. Over time, the savings compound and grow. When you decide to start drawing from that money, it becomes a tax-free income stream.

Why Get to Zero?

Right now, I know you must be thinking, "What's so important about getting to zero percent taxes?" For most households, taxes are the number-one destroyer of wealth, and they don't even know it! For example, there's a huge freight train sitting in most people's 401(k) accounts waiting to crash into them when it's time to cash out their IRAs, and they haven't even thought of it. It's a combination of issues that can end up being problematic.

- Compounding growth is good, yes, but it will also result in compounding taxes. Your tax bill becomes larger the more your money grows.
- If you want to take social security when you retire, as most of us do, there's a little-known fact called provisional income, which we talked about in Chapter 10. If you make withdrawals from this account, you might trigger provisional income, which, at the time of this writing, would now make the taxation on your social security disbursements a whopping 85 percent.
- Laws can change between now and the time you retire, which can really screw you over by the time you're ready to retire.

However, the cool thing is that once you've got a deep understanding—emotionally, physically, mentally—of what is happening with the tax system, then you'll realize that the power is in your hands. You get to control how much you pay in taxes.

Real estate income is one of the things triggering provisional income, but you have more control over the taxes you pay because the IRS considers real estate owners *important to the economy*—giving you the opportunity to cut down your tax burden through straight-line or accelerated depreciation and 1031 exchanges. Real estate is its own beast, allowing you so much leverage that it's something I definitely would encourage you to explore.

One way that you can do this is by following the strategy put forth by David McKnight that I mentioned earlier in this chapter. In his plan, from your income (however you earn it, but we're hoping to get you to the business owner/investor side of the equation) you are able to finance your lifestyle, then put aside money into your savings, which goes into one of the three buckets.

- **The Taxable Bucket:** This is your emergency fund, and anything above six months' income should be shifted from this bucket immediately. (You can go up to twelve months if that's what your lifestyle necessitates or it helps you sleep better at night.)
- **The Tax-Deferred Bucket:** This is where you keep just enough so that your required minimum distribution (RMD) falls below your

personal tax exemption (which, as of 2023, is $12,950 for an individual or $25,900 for a married couple). For most people, currently, that's about $500,000, according to McKnight in *The Power of Zero*.[19] Anything above $500,000 will most likely trigger an RMD above your personal tax exemption, thus triggering provisional income tax, resulting in double taxation of any social security you may be eligible for.

- **The Tax-Free Bucket:** Any money above what's required for your taxable income in your tax-deferred bucket is what you'll shift into something like a cash flow life insurance policy or real estate.

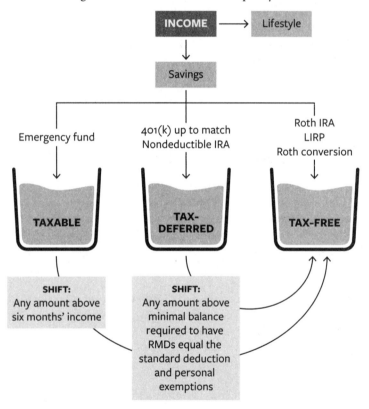

So where does that leave you if you want to get into the zero percent tax bracket? Consider shifting your assets by working with a qualified

---

19 McKnight, *The Power of Zero*.

financial professional who can help you create a plan and convert your assets to ensure you don't pay unnecessary taxes. Here are a few questions you can ask any financial professional that you're considering hiring, in order to figure out if you're working with the right person.

1. How can we identify all of my income streams in retirement and create a plan to not trigger provisional income when I retire?
2. What's the plan to convert my assets prior to retirement?
3. How can we use today's tax code to execute a "Power of Zero" plan?
4. What are the drawbacks if I wait to execute this plan?

The answers to these questions will help you to determine the best plan for your retirement that will not only benefit you, but also your family overall.

YOUR CHAPTER ACTION PLAN

1. Calculate the Investment Index for all of your existing accounts and investments.
2. Using the results, create an action plan to maximize your Investment Index.
3. Consult a tax professional to better understand how provisional income might impact you at retirement.
4. Create an action plan to move closer to zero taxes.

Real Stories of Money for Tomorrow
PRINCIPLES IN ACTION

Dan Handford, managing partner, PassiveInvesting.com

At the same time as starting our family in 2011, my wife and I also started four nonsurgical orthopedic medical clinics in South Carolina.

Over the next five years, our medical clinics were growing year-over-year and producing a healthy amount of cash flow as they were debt-free. This significant cash flow was great, but we also had to pay a ton of federal income tax to Uncle Sam throughout the year. I'm talking about large six-figure checks—every quarter.

Business was great—but we had a significant tax problem that would erode our wealth.

So, we started to research how wealthy people pay little to no taxes, even with high incomes. As you can imagine, real estate was that ticket to help reduce our taxable liability with the help of depreciation.

We started researching real estate investing to fill our knowledge gaps and found resources like BiggerPockets. We also spent many hours consuming podcasts, YouTube videos, and real estate investing books, as well as touring potential investment properties.

However, my wife and I were working full-time in the medical clinics and raising four kids under the age of twelve. We felt we just didn't have the free time to confidently acquire an asset. Or so we told ourselves!

Two years passed in this research phase of our journey before I attended a business conference with a friend, and I heard one of the speakers talk about how I needed to become the "general" in my business. I thought to myself, "I am the general!" But as the speaker continued, I realized that I was not the general. It was during a 3 a.m. conversation with my friend at that conference that I finally realized I was acting mostly on the front lines of my business, putting out fires throughout the day to keep myself busy rather than making the necessary corporate hires so I could focus on what I needed to do to eliminate my tax problem for myself and my family.

Energized by my realization, that weekend my wife and I decided to make a strategic decision that would allow me to step out of the day-to-day operations of the medical clinics. The next person I called was our COO and told him that I was promoting him to CEO, and I would stay on as president. We would still have a monthly corporate meeting to review the KPIs and make sure that our vision for the clinics was still being carried out, even with me not being in the clinics full-time. I was confident this business restructure and successful transition out of our business (as my wife joined me too) would allow me to focus on making our real estate investing a reality.

With our sights now set on real estate investing, I knew I didn't want to start small, so I decided to start my own real estate syndication company. The first thing I did was start investing as a limited partner in a few syndications with other operators. Then I hired a mentor, who helped me reduce my learning curve. Soon after, I started Handford Capital and partnered with two operating groups to help me build my track record and credibility. In no time, I met my business partner, Danny Randazzo, through a mutual mentor, and we merged our companies in 2018 into PassiveInvesting.com. As of 2022, we have partnered with over 2,000 passive investors to acquire more than $1.7 billion in assets.

Needless to say, business is going great—and now, so are our taxes.

The depreciation benefit from our real estate holdings has continued to build up year-over-year to the point where we have eliminated our taxable liability in subsequent years. These tax savings allow us to create velocity with our money and invest more in our real estate and our business. This was the golden ticket that we were looking for—the whole reason we need to step out of our comfort zone to make a difference.

Another benefit of starting our private equity real estate investment firm is that we have been able to teach our children about finances and investing. Our rule for our children is that they must earn $1,000 before they can invest in an offering. Once they make that $1,000, they can invest in our real estate offerings alongside us. Our oldest daughter, age twelve, has saved enough to invest in a couple of our multifamily offerings as well as our express car washes. Our son, age eleven, has invested in an offering that has seven express car washes, with some of the businesses close to where we live (he counts the cars in the vacuum areas every time we pass by them).

Sound money principles on how to create, keep, and grow my wealth are something that I wish my parents had learned when I was younger, so they could have passed that knowledge along to me. But I am the parent now. And I am looking forward to teaching and witnessing my children's investing journey as they learn and grow.

SECTION V
Passing Wealth On

CHAPTER 14

Building Your Multigenerational Wealth Plan

I can't paint, but I can trace the Mona Lisa.

—UNKNOWN

In the previous chapters, we've taken a deep dive into what you can do to transform your current financial situation and create the life you've always dreamed of—regardless of your age, marital status, where you live, or where you're starting from.

But it would be remiss of me not to help you figure out one of the most important parts of creating wealth, and quite frankly where so many people fail: building their multigenerational wealth plan so they can pass their wealth on to the next generation effectively and efficiently. Essentially, this is where we talk about how to … well … *die*.

Death Is Inevitable but Poor Planning Isn't

Imagine for a moment that you get a call one morning. It's early in the morning, and your house is still; maybe your kids and your partner haven't even woken up yet. You pick up the phone, only to find out that a loved one has suddenly passed away in the night.

You know that this loved one has been struggling with health issues for a while. They might have had dementia or another illness that limited their ability to take care of themselves.

Despite this, you and this loved one haven't been very close over the past few years. Things haven't been rosy between the two of you for a variety of reasons. But upon receiving the call that they've died, you are now on the biggest emotional roller coaster of your life because you know you are the executor or trustee of their estate.

The problem? You know next to nothing about their estate, nor where the original will or trust is, let alone where any other documents and assets are. What happens by the end of that day, after that earth-shattering phone call, is that you're handed a set of keys to a distressed home—filled to the eaves with old, outdated things—that is in massive need of repairs and is on the brink of foreclosure because your loved one didn't understand how to handle their finances or final affairs.

In this situation, you find yourself dealing with two insurmountable tasks: the swarm of emotions that come from losing a loved one, and the potential traumas associated with settling their estate and probably going through a very public probate to do it.

This scene sounds like something out of a film, doesn't it? Maybe the beginning of a tragic drama. But this sort of situation isn't far-fetched. It happens to people every single day. It happened to me.

To be honest, I should have known that April 19 was going to be a day like that for me because of how it started: I stuck my hand into the pocket of one of my coats that had been hanging *in my closet* and got stung by a yellow jacket. A sign of things soon to come.

Still, I was hopeful for the day. I headed down to Denver to meet with the CEO of BiggerPockets to discuss ways that we could work together—quite a big deal, considering that I was just ramping up my real estate mentoring business. But somehow, we got our timing mixed up, and the meeting was rescheduled.

I got into my car to drive thirty minutes back home and picked up my phone to call my mother—it had been more than a month since we'd talked. She didn't pick up, and I was fed up. I was more than a thousand miles away from her, and her denial regarding her alcohol-related dementia diagnosis didn't make things any easier. I was upset, of course—so upset that I was determined to get her to talk to me that day, even if it meant calling the police to perform a wellness check on her.

That's when I found out that she had passed.

To say it was traumatic is an understatement. I can't tell you how many times I've heard stories like this. I wouldn't wish a situation like this on anyone, and yet it happens so often. Processing grief in and of itself is difficult, but to throw in a tangled financial situation and the chaos of a poorly organized estate? It's the perfect storm that could push anyone past the brink of what they're able to handle.

However, I learned a lot during this experience, and that's what I'm going to share with you now.

Building Your "I Love You Plan"

Initially I called this plan the "Cover Your Ass" plan. After all, when you pass, you can hand your family a binder with "everything" in it, and you'd effectively be covering your own ass. But after experiencing it myself, I realize there's so much more to it than just that. Your family is going to be dealing with an avalanche of emotions—primarily grief.

They can't read your mind. They won't be able to know what you were thinking when you organized your estate the way you did. They'll be dealing with the things said, and even more so, the things unsaid. Organizing your affairs and compiling your final wishes isn't really about you at the end of the day, *because you'll be gone*. It's about showing your family how much you love them by making it easier for them to settle your affairs after your passing.

I've broken it down into a plan that you can start building on right now, called your "I Love You Plan." The things in this plan are the kinds of things that an attorney will tell you—for a fee, of course, after you've stumbled into a roadblock with the probate or estate settlement process. I've synthesized all of this information into an easy-to-use, fillable spreadsheet that you can download at https://get.biggerpockets.com/whitney/.

I'll tell you all about it, and why it's so important to create this plan.

Prepare for Your Passing: The Legal Side

The first part of your I Love You Plan involves letting your family know your wishes. Yes, this can be communicated verbally, but it is most important your wishes are put into legal writing, making challenges to your wishes less likely—as well as less likely for the courts to step in and change a decision you have made. This process is known as *estate planning*.

Estate planning consists of three steps: 1) planning for your incapacity, 2) planning to transfer assets using a will or trust, and 3) protecting the inheritance as it passes to heirs.

Step 1: Preparing for Your Incapacity

Many people think they can postpone the estate planning process until they have accumulated assets, have children, or are older. That couldn't be further from the truth. If you remember back to our discussion in Chapter 6, incapacitation could be one of the largest drains to your wealth—especially for the unprepared. Incapacitation means a person is no longer able to care for themselves or their affairs. It could be permanent or for a short period of time, and it can extend to affairs such as property, financial, and legal management. As such, everyone should prepare now to be incapacitated, because we just don't know if or when it will happen to us.

Here are the documents you need.

- **An advance health care directive, also known as a living will,** helps guard against a sudden change in your health condition draining your accounts. This set of legal documents includes a health care power of attorney, living will, and HIPAA authorization. Through these documents, you define what actions should be taken for your health if you are no longer able to make decisions for yourself due to illness or incapacity. If you become unconscious or mentally incompetent, a health care power of attorney allows you to appoint someone to make medical care decisions on your behalf. With a signed HIPAA authorization and living will directive, medical records will be accessible to your designated agent, and health care professionals will be able to speak with your agent to make informed decisions on your behalf. This differs from a *durable power of attorney,* which allows your agent to make broad legal decisions on your behalf. It is a good idea to work with an attorney to draft a durable power of attorney and appoint an agent to be in charge of your financial decisions while you are incapacitated.

Here is a pro wealth tip: If you have kids over the age of eighteen, have them complete an advance health care directive including a HIPAA authorization so medical professionals can share private health care information with you, and you can help manage your kids' health care needs. Again, no one ever plans to be incapacitated.

Step 2: Preparing to Pass Your Assets On

There are two options available to you to pass your assets on to the next generation. One option is reactive estate planning (a will), while the other option is proactive estate planning (a living trust). Ideally, we all want to be proactive in our planning; however, the key point here is to ensure you have at least one of these estate planning options in place now. Let's explore the differences.

- **A will** allows you to define your last wishes rather than the state probate courts deciding. If you draft a will, you have not ensured a smooth way to pass assets on to your heirs. Upon your death, anything titled to your name will immediately transfer to your "estate." Your personal representative will file your will with the probate courts. They will work with the courts to legally distribute assets from your estate to your beneficiaries according to your will, once all interested parties (beneficiaries, beneficiary spouses, creditors, etc.) have been notified. This entire process is known as *probate*—which is a very public process. It also can be a lengthy process, with the average probate taking nine to eighteen months. Many people choose to use a will to pass along assets, since the cost to set up a will is very low compared to that of a trust—hundreds of dollars compared to thousands of dollars. Setting up a will is only one part of the process, though. And the cost of taking a will through probate can cost $4,000 or more. If you do not have kids, or if your kids are grown and you have a simple estate (e.g., a home, car, one retirement account, and a checking account, all valued less than $1 million and all heirs are on good terms), creating a simple will may suffice. You can use LegalShield, Nolo.com, Rocket Lawyer, or your own lawyer, depending on the complexity of the will you would like to set up.

- **A living trust with a pour-over will** allows you to bequeath your estate (especially financial, real estate, and business interests) without going through probate proceedings. There are many other advantages as well, such as designating care for young kids, providing asset protection, protecting assets from a previous marriage, and more! Why is this process smoother? When you transfer your assets into a living trust prior to passing, there is no gap in ownership for those assets. However, *transferring the assets is the key.* Many living trusts have been created and not funded. In that case, the living trust has to be funded through a pour-over will upon your passing. The benefit is that assets will move into your trust, and the trust will govern how those assets will be managed. But there is a catch—since there was a gap in ownership for those assets that were not in the trust previously, the pour-over will does have to go through probate, which, again, is a very public and expensive process. Your best course of action here is to move all of your assets into the trust upon its formation and maintain it regularly.

Before we move on, there's a common misconception that you need to have a living trust to name guardianship over small children—that a will won't cut it. That isn't entirely correct. If you decide on a will instead of a trust, be certain to complete a separate document designating the guardian of your children. If you have a living trust, you can name guardians within the trust document. In either case, the courts will have to approve your named guardian(s) to ensure they are willing and capable of taking care of any children at the time of your passing.

Regardless of which avenue appeals to you now, it's worthwhile to sit down with a good estate attorney to decide which option is the best for your personal situation. Many people find a will suits their needs if their estate is relatively small (say, valued less than $1 million); is made up of bank and retirement accounts; and their heirs are older, are on good terms, and in a position in life to manage the inheritance well. If one or more of those factors don't apply, you should strongly consider a living trust so you have greater control over how your assets are distributed and managed, as well as limiting the chances of your estate being openly contested in court. More importantly, if you are reading this book, I bet you are committed to growing your assets and generating wealth for generations to come, which means a living trust may better suit your needs.

When is the best time to plan … ?

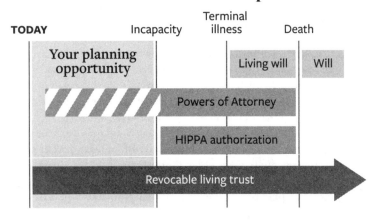

Step 3: Protecting the Inheritance as It Passes

As you draft your legal documents to plan for your incapacity and to pass your assets on, you will want to think through some key questions to set up your heirs/beneficiaries for success. This is a key step to ensuring any assets you have passed on go to the right people at the right time in the right situations.

I recently attended an estate planning retreat where the speaker shared a shocking statistic: In their practice experience, beneficiaries under the age of thirty-five generally have spent their entire inheritance in less than eighteen months. We will talk more in Chapter 15 on how to train and prepare your heirs to be good stewards of the wealth you choose to pass on.

But how many stories have you heard about kids receiving large trusts and blowing through all of the money due to excessive spending, excessive debts, or substance abuse? Or an estranged spouse popping back into the picture to contest "their share"? Or family feuds occurring because a second spouse gained control of the estate instead of the heirs?

While you can't (and probably shouldn't) account for every possible situation that could occur, it's a good exercise to think through possible sticky situations in your family and put some parameters in place. Ironing out these details now and updating these decisions regularly could save thousands (in some families, millions) in legal time and court costs—keeping assets intact according to *your* wishes and setting up your family for multigenerational wealth.

Questions to think through with proper legal counsel include:

- Who is the best person to make key decisions regarding your health, finances, estate, and children? You may designate multiple agents.
- How will assets be divided among the heirs/beneficiaries?
- If you choose a trust:
  - Who will manage your trust now and when you pass?
  - How will your beneficiaries receive their assets?
  - When will beneficiaries receive assets?
  - How will the trust treat other interested parties (e.g., your child's spouse, ex-spouses, kids by marriage)?
  - How will the trust treat beneficiary special-case situations (e.g., age requirements, education requirements, job requirements, excessive spending and debts, substance abuse situations)?
  - If beneficiaries are young children, do you need to consider appointing a corporate trustee or trust protector until they are willing and able to take over?

Keep in mind this chapter is not a substitute for legal advice or an exhaustive account of which estate planning document to choose, but to arm you with the core principles that will yield the greatest results. Of course, there are other fancy legal maneuvers discussed in achieving financial freedom, but most of those strategies are for people who have more than $10 million in net assets in their estate. Even those fancy maneuvers have the intention of ensuring your estate passes on according to your wishes.

How to Avoid Common Pitfalls

Once you have worked with your legal professional to get your legal documents in place, follow the steps below to help avoid common pitfalls with estate settlements.

- Sign and notarize your documents (if required in your state) with two witnesses present. Ideally, your witnesses should be people who know you and will vouch for your state of mind at the time you signed your documents, but are disinterested third parties who wouldn't stand to benefit from your passing.
- When signing your documents, be sure to sign all original documents in **bright blue ink**, so there is no mistake on what is an original versus a copy. Bonus points if you initial all pages in blue ink as well.
- Let everyone who may be impacted by your estate know that documents have been drafted and signed, as well as that an executor/executrix (in the case of a will) or trustee (in the case of a trust) has been named.
- Ensure that your executor/trustee has a copy of all documents and that they know any and all procedures needed to access the original documents when you pass.
- If you choose to put the original copy of your legal documents in a bank safety deposit box, ensure that your executor/trustee is either named as a co-owner of the bank deposit box or knows the procedure to gain access to it after your death *but before probate is opened.* Most banks will give a one-time pass for an executor/trustee to get into the box to remove a will or trust, but will require a copy of the will or trust and death certificate to do so.
- Be sure to advise your executor/trustee to not hastily notify banks of your death. If they do this, the banks will freeze your accounts and not let any transactions take place until any legal proceedings have been settled, which can take months. This will not be helpful,

as in an ideal situation you will want to have autopay for bills set up from a well-funded account (ideally with six months of reserves set aside), meaning your estate will continue to function and pay for itself while your executor/trustee navigates either opening probate and/or settling your affairs. Bonus points if you have your checking account linked to your savings to handle any overdrafts that may occur.

By putting these plans in place for your assets, you'll save both your executor/trustee and beneficiaries time, money, and heartache while they get things in order and execute your wishes.

Preparing Your Assets: Your Estate/Emergency Binder

Creating a will or trust is often the first thing that people consider when they think about planning for the transfer of their estate. However, I've found so many things are left out—they forget to include key documents, information, and even account login information that's essential to ensuring that their executor/trustee is able to complete their tasks set out in the will or trust smoothly. A fillable copy of an Estate/Emergency Binder is included in my I Love You Plan download at https://get.biggerpockets.com/whitney/.

An Estate/Emergency Binder is exactly what it sounds like—a dual-purpose binder filled with everything that your executor/trustee needs to know to locate and settle assets with ease. It can also come into play before you've even passed, like in the case of a serious accident that has left you without the ability to make decisions for yourself. Completing the template may feel like a heavy lift the first time you do it—especially if being organized doesn't come naturally to you—but you won't regret having all of this information at your fingertips. So be sure to sit annually (at a minimum) to make any updates to your binder and keep the information current.

In your Estate/Emergency Binder, you want to make sure to complete several lists.

- **List all your banking, investment, and insurance accounts.** It may also be a wise decision to ensure that all of your bank accounts that aren't titled to your trust (if you have one) have a listed designee in the Paid on Death clause. This will allow the account's assets to seamlessly transfer to the person listed as Paid on Death and bypass most probate courts.

- **List all your loans, mortgages, and credit card accounts.** Ideally, you'd want to have your executor/trustee already listed as an authorized contact (very different from an authorized user) on all these accounts. This will allow them to report your passing to the company in a timely manner in case it takes a few days/weeks to secure a death certificate.
- **List the location of any deeds, titles, certificates, and collections** (jewelry, coins, metals, art, etc.), as well as any insurance policies (like homeowner's, auto, life, and accidental death), and store a copy with your Estate/Emergency Binder as well as with your original trust or will. This will make locating assets a breeze for your executor/trustee. If you feel comfortable, you can secure these items in a locked location along with your original documents.
- **List all your utilities, homeowner's insurance, auto insurance accounts, and any other service accounts** (like lawn care, house-cleaning, etc.). This will help anyone handling your affairs to settle your accounts with ease without having to research who you were doing business with and locate the account. Additionally, indicate in your Estate/Emergency Binder whether or not this account will be needed after you pass. For example, homeowner's insurance is a necessity, and your lawn will become overgrown if not cared for. Bonus points: If your executor/trustee will be handling a home after your passing, ensure lawn service doesn't stop. You do not want to advertise to everyone that your home is no longer occupied after you pass.
- **List bills that would need to be paid after death and set them to autopay to be drafted from your bank account, not credit cards.** Things like your water, electric, and auto insurance shouldn't be put on credit. By linking these bills to your well-funded bank account, your estate can pay these necessary bills while your executor/trustee is navigating the legal system—again, saving them time, money, and heartache.
- **List all of your account logins and passwords in an encrypted password vault** like LastPass.com or 1Password. While this isn't a must, this can be a safe way to pass along sensitive login information to your executor/trustee or surviving family members. With a family account, you can program the vault to pass along to anyone you designate as long as certain parameters are met. Once again, this saves your loved ones time, money, and heartache.

In my mother's case, her life wasn't set up like this at all. Her credit cards were shut down for nonpayment months before her death, and her bank account was immediately frozen after she died, since I was not listed on the account as an owner or as the Paid on Death designee. I had to not only locate all of her accounts (by navigating the piles of documents and mail in her home and getting on the phone for hours on end to negotiate access), but I also had to pay for all of these bills out of pocket with no prospect of reimbursement until after her estate had been through probate—which can take six months or longer to navigate, even for the most organized estate.

This could prove to be a real emotional and financial nightmare for your executor/trustee. That's why this chapter is all about saving your loved ones time, heartache, and money when settling your assets. Moreover, you may avoid big legal expenses if your estate can be settled quickly and seamlessly.

Keep in mind that setting up a system like the Estate/Emergency Binder can also prove useful should you ever have to flee for an emergency (like a hurricane, fire, or flood). You can simply grab this binder and have most (if not all) of your assets with you.

Eight Additional Ways to Make Life Easier for You and Your Executor/Trustee/Heirs When You Pass

While these are not a necessity for your Estate/Emergency Binder, including them in your final wishes will make it *light-years* easier for your executor/trustee to handle your estate. Here are some of my best tips for keeping the transition smooth.

- **Train your executor/trustee on where everything is.** You want them to be up to date on how to access your information and what your high-level wishes are. Know you can change your mind at any point; just be sure to keep your executor/trustee informed.
- **Appraise any expensive jewelry, coins, and papers and securely lock them up.** When you pass there may be MANY people passing through your home, and you don't want to lose anything important to sticky fingers.
- **Interview probate/estate attorneys and leave a short list for your executor/trustee to choose from.** Better yet, you can even find one you really like and retain them at a discounted fee, saving your executor/trustee the need to find a way to pay for it while your assets are being settled.

- **Plan (and pay for) your funeral service.** This can be a huge gift to your loved ones. If you go this route, leave this documentation with the original will, and a copy with the executor/trustee. You'll be able to have your final wishes respected, and your executor/trustee doesn't have to figure out how to pay for it. If you opt for a cremation with a family-led service, you can even choose to use a mortuary service rather than a funeral home in order to lower the costs.
- **Make a list of who gets your belongings, and leave this information with the original trust or will for your executor/trustee.** If you are making a hard decision about not leaving someone money or belongings, take the time to write a letter regarding *why* you are making this choice and seal it with your documents. Don't assume that people won't get hurt feelings or will automatically accept the choices you made. This simple step can save some families steep legal fees from contesting assets.
- **Reduce your "footprint" as you get older to take some workload off your family and executor/trustee.** In Sweden, there is a tradition called "death cleaning."[20] This would involve cleaning out your home yourself, reducing your files, digitizing your photos, and giving away items that you can't use or maintain anymore to family and friends—all in the name of reducing your footprint as you age. You can do this yourself, or hire a move manager to assist and contract an auction service to sell the items your family doesn't want. You get the funds to spend as you wish now, and the enjoyment of a clutter-free home.
- **List your preferred vendors that you trust, as repairs may need to be done on your property prior to sale.** While your executor/trustee can always find a general contractor or handyman to assist with any property repairs, think about leaving a list of trusted vendors you already work with like a handyman, roofer, plumber, HVAC specialist, electrician, yard and sprinkler maintenance services, and a realtor to get your house sold.
- **If you have a lot of belongings, or just don't know where to start when it comes to breaking everything down**, it's fine to let your executor/trustee know that your house can be sold "as-is" to an investor with all your belongings—it will probably sell for less, but it could be a huge emotional savings for your family.

---

20 Sarah DiGiulio, "What is 'Swedish death cleaning' and should you be doing it?" NBC News BETTER, November 7, 2017, https://www.nbcnews.com/better/health/what-swedish-death-cleaning-should-you-be-doing-it-ncna816511.

One of the biggest things that I can't stress enough is that so many of these plans aren't meant to be made by someone who is dying or on the brink of death. These decisions are meant to be made when you're healthy and with a clear mind, so that, should the inevitable happen, you can be confident that you made the best decision for the preservation of your family's wealth and emotional well-being.

What If You End Up Being an Executor/Executrix or Trustee?

We've talked a lot about what to do in order to make the life of your executor/trustee easier, but what if *you* end up being named as the executor or trustee of a loved one's will or trust? You know I've been in those shoes before—and they are *definitely* large shoes to fill. Here are some of the best tips I can give you.

1. First of all, *breathe.* You just lost someone important to you. It's okay to grieve the loss of your loved one. As the executor/trustee of somebody's estate, it will take time, even with the best planning. So, there's no rush to get it done all at once. You need to make sure you allow yourself to mourn. If I had to prioritize, here are a few things that I'd say have to be done rather quickly.
   - Arrange immediate care of any minors, dependents, and pets
   - Set up funeral or mortuary arrangements to get the death certificate process going
   - Locate the original will or trust, asset documents, and assets.
   - Ensure that the death certificate is finalized—this will trigger social security payments to stop, and creditors will be notified.
   - Create video documentation of all real property and physical assets
   - Forward the deceased's mail to your home
2. Once you have your bearings, next:
   - Contact the estate/probate attorney, if necessary, to apprise them of the situation.
   - Open the probate proceedings.
   - Create an inventory of all assets and bills. Hopefully, a well-thought-out Estate/Emergency Binder was left for you. Keep track (with receipts) of anything you have to pay for yourself in order to administer the estate, so you can be reimbursed later.
   - If going through probate, secure your letters of testamentary.

- Convert the deceased's accounts that are not payable on death to an estate account. If they are already payable on death and you are the beneficiary, confirm with the bank and your attorney that you are free to use the account as is to pay bills.

These tips can make your role as an executor/trustee infinitely easier, and much less stressful.

Building a Board of Advisors for Your Life

The next step of building your multigenerational wealth plan involves building a board of advisors—otherwise known as a network that can help both you and your executor/trustee if it comes down to it. From my own experience, having your own network of advisors is invaluable when it comes to creating and sustaining your wealth plan across multiple generations.

First, you'll want to have your core board that you should be meeting with fairly regularly—at a minimum of once per year, or before you make a large investment or transaction decision.

1. **An insurance agent/professional:** A good insurance agent will also be able to offer advice on how to reduce your risk of liability. This person will help you coordinate the best coverage to protect your assets, like:
     - Property and casualty insurance
     - Medical insurance
     - Disability insurance
     - Life insurance

2. **A legal professional:** Working with a lawyer or legal professional will help you navigate the legalities of your investment and estate strategy. This is especially important if you want to invest in assets like real estate, as there are several legal considerations that must be taken into account. This person can also help you review the legal documents to ensure your investment is legally sound, review your personal legal structure, advise you on the best way to structure your investment, and assist with any disputes that may arise. Ideally, your legal professional should have a background in the assets you primarily invest in (real estate, securities, businesses, etc.). Bonus points if they work closely with a tax group as well.

3. **A tax professional:** An accountant or tax professional is one of the most important players on your team. They can help you minimize your taxes (leveraging depreciation and accelerated depreciation) and maximize your profits. This individual can also help you manage your income and expenses, prepare your return, keep track of your investments, and help with any tax-related issues that may arise. It is best to source a tax professional with experience in the assets you primarily invest in (real estate, securities, businesses, etc.). Bonus points if they do proactive tax planning with you. The best time to find them is *before* you invest!

4. **A strategic advisor or mentor:** A strategic advisor or mentor—like me at AshWealth.com—can help you identify your goals, your risk tolerance, and your investing timelines. Once that initial groundwork is set, this person can provide guidance and feedback on which investments would be a good fit for your portfolio to grow your wealth over time, helping you keep on track toward your life and wealth goals.

Once you've created your core board of advisors and figured out the type of business/investments you want to get involved in, that's when you start to assemble the rest of your ancillary team, like bookkeepers, agents, lenders, cash flow life insurance professionals, and personal bankers.

Creating this advisory board is all about helping you get your multigenerational wealth plan off the ground. Meeting with them regularly as your plan grows will help you to stay on track and level up. Think of them as a sounding board for your decisions to make sure there are no holes or pitfalls on the path you're about to take.

However, as you grow your estate, you may need to replace members of your advisory board to bring on new skills and up your game (e.g., your cousin the insurance agent may not be the best fit anymore, or the family friend who has always done your taxes may not be the best person to assist you with real estate–related tax matters).

YOUR CHAPTER ACTION PLAN

1. Consult with a legal professional to draft your legal documents.
   - Advanced medical directives and powers of attorney
   - A will or a living trust with a pour-over will
   - Address any special inheritance protection needs in your legal documents
2. Complete your Estate/Emergency Binder template.
   - Store all original legal documents and assets in a secure location.
3. Train your executor/trustee on your final wishes and how to access all originals of your documents in the event of your death.
4. Review the eight ways you could make life easier for you and your heirs when you pass.
5. Build your core four team members who will serve as your trusted board of advisors. Remember, your advisory board should grow with you as your goals and portfolio grow.

Real Stories of Money for Tomorrow
PRINCIPLES IN ACTION

The Power of Purposeful Estate Planning and Avoiding Unforeseen Consequences—Peter C. Osman, partner, attorney, and counselor-at-law, Borakove | Osman LLC

We all recognize the importance of estate planning for the well-being of our loved ones. However, the truth is that many of us shy away from discussions about incapacity, asset distribution, and our own mortality. The result? Too many individuals and couples defer these conversations indefinitely, leading to missed opportunities to secure and safeguard their family's future.

While estate planning conversations may not be the most pleasant, they are crucial. Often, people avoid these discussions because they associate estate planning solely with death, incapacity, and finances. But what if we shifted our perspective? What if estate planning were about protection, wealth and values preservation, and opportunities for the next generation? By reframing the conversation, we can make estate planning engaging and appealing, helping us move beyond the fear of death to focus on benefiting those we cherish most.

Below, we'll explore the transformative power of thoughtful estate planning by contrasting the experiences of two families—families who have come through the doors of my practice. We'll examine the outcomes of their approaches to estate planning, shedding light on both the financial and interpersonal implications—or repercussions—of their choices.

Family 1: Missed Opportunities and Their Repercussions

Dave and Kathy's story mirrors the situations of many couples. Despite hearing about the importance of estate planning from friends and family, they believed it wasn't necessary for them. They thought their situation was simple, and they assumed everything would "sort itself out." Sadly, this mindset led to a series of challenges and consequences.

- **Incapacity Crisis:** When Dave suffered a stroke and was left incapacitated, Kathy faced numerous obstacles. Lacking advance medical directives to be able to make medical decisions on Dave's behalf, Kathy had to navigate a cumbersome court-based guardianship process just to get the power to make important medical decisions for Dave. As if the court-mandated guardian ad litem evaluations weren't intrusive enough, the process also incurred legal fees of $6,000 and left the family in limbo for months.

- **Asset Distribution Challenges:** Following Dave's passing, Kathy again encountered difficulties accessing assets titled solely in his name. Since they lived in a communal property state and had no prenuptial arrangement in place, their assumption was that everything would automatically pass to Kathy upon his death. This was proven wrong—leading to the necessity of opening a probate. This process was costly, involving legal fees of over $10,000 and taking more than a year to complete. Furthermore, all of this information was now a matter of public record.

- **Strained Family Relationships:** Despite her experiences with probate, Kathy never completed any proactive planning with her estate. Ten years later, Kathy died and left her three children to figure out their next steps. The probate process to settle Kathy's estate strained the relationships among the children. Disputes arose and sibling bonds were fractured due to misunderstandings and a lack of communication.
- **Unforeseen Divorce Complications:** Bruce, one of Kathy's children, experienced unexpected complications during his divorce. Despite inheriting a substantial amount from his mother's estate, he made a costly mistake by comingling the inheritance with jointly titled accounts, resulting in his ex-wife being awarded half of the inheritance in the divorce settlement.

Unfortunately, Dave and Kathy's legacy—now Bruce's legacy—was marred by missed opportunities, a lack of understanding, and inadequate planning. Their assumption that their estate was "simple" led to financial losses, strained relationships, and unintended consequences.

Family 2: The Benefits of Comprehensive Estate Planning

In contrast, John and Laura approached estate planning with a proactive mindset. Despite considering their situation to be relatively straightforward as well, they recognized the importance of proper planning and engaged in a comprehensive estate planning process. After weighing the options, they chose a revocable living trust, and the results were significantly different from Dave and Kathy's results.

- **Smooth Incapacity Transition:** When John faced a heart attack, Laura was able to seamlessly make important decisions for him using the health care power of attorney. The need for costly guardianship proceedings was avoided, and Laura could act on his behalf immediately.
- **Efficient Asset Transition:** Following John's passing, Laura didn't have to navigate the complexities of probate, since all of the assets in their joint living trust continued for her benefit. She simply had to notify the banks of John's passing and have him removed as a trustee and beneficiary of the trust.
- **Structured Succession:** Laura's passing eight years later also didn't require probate due to the trust structure. Their children, well-informed about their roles as successor trustees, efficiently managed trust administration.
- **Informed Trust Administration:** The absence of court paperwork, creditors' claims, and hearings streamlined trust administration. Siblings collab-

orated to coordinate the administration process, maintaining transparent communication—and assets were distributed in nine months.

- **Protected Inheritance:** The inheritance structure, outlined in the revocable trust, ensured that their children would inherit their share of the trust in an ongoing trust for their benefit. This structure protected the inheritance from potential risks such as divorce, lawsuits, or bankruptcy.
- **Divorce Shield:** Kelly, one of the children, faced divorce years later. Her inheritance, protected within the trust and never comingled with marital assets, remained untouched by the divorce proceedings.

The contrast between Bruce and Kathy's situation and John and Laura's situation highlights the profound impact of deliberate estate planning. Even in relatively straightforward scenarios, investing effort, time, and resources into comprehensive estate planning resulted in vastly divergent outcomes.

Estate planning encompasses more than preparing for death, incapacity, and financial matters. It's about securing protection, upholding values, and creating avenues for future generations. By taking the initiative to create a comprehensive estate plan, families can avoid missed opportunities, financial setbacks, strained relationships, and legal complexities. Approaching estate planning as an empowering tool enables individuals to secure their legacy, protect their loved ones, and face the future with confidence.

=== CHAPTER 15 ===

Why Most Families Fail at Passing Wealth On

Financial knowledge isn't power—
it's potential power.
You have to take action.

When I started my studies on wealth creation, the Chinese proverb "Wealth does not pass three generations" puzzled me. Why do most families fail at passing their wealth on to their children and their children's children? Well, as it turns out, I didn't have to look far for the answer to that question—it was sitting right there in my own family.

I told you the Tale of Two Grandfathers earlier; now it's time to tell you the Tale of Two Sons. Both of them were sons of Grandfather #2. Their father had some sense of how to create money, keep it, and grow it. Both sons attended college, got married, had one or more children, were very successful in their careers for over forty years, and invested in the stock market for retirement. They had the "perfect American life"—the traditional narrative that we're sold as the best way to live our lives.

But when it came time for retirement, that's when their paths diverged. Son #1 had health issues almost ending in bankruptcy (for full disclosure, he was my dad). However, Son #2 started investing in mineral rights and then fell into real estate investing at age 60, when a friend of his left him a self-storage facility and liquor store in his will. In this story, there are two failures already.

- My grandfather, though he was money-savvy and learned to invest and kept investing even in his later years, never taught his sons the fundamental building blocks of wealth. (Ideally, Son #2 shouldn't have gotten to age 60 before leaning into what his father had done to build his own wealth.)

- Neither son knew the fundamentals of wealth, and that impacted their lives, and they weren't able to pass on that information to their children—yes, I'm talking about me and my cousins. I didn't learn anything about growing and protecting wealth until I stumbled into it when I bought my first house.

Because you're reading this book, however, this is your chance to be the transitional character in your narrative. *You* can be the one who changes things for your family, the one who creates the environment, knowledge, and legacy that will benefit your bloodline for generations to come. You have to accept this challenge, though I'm pretty sure you have if you've made it this far in the book. **Only you can break this cycle of** *financial incapability*—**where someone has access to the financial knowledge needed to succeed, but for one reason or another fails to act on it.**

You need to be the one to educate yourself *and* your successors on their mindset, their skills, and their network. This book is an amazing start, a framework for what you need to succeed, but you'll still have to do the work. Financial knowledge isn't power, it's potential power. *You have to take action.* You need to create your wealthy balance sheet, root out all of the things that would erode your wealth, grow your wealth through your investment vehicles of choice, and pass your knowledge and strategies down to the next generation.

Here are some action steps to take to ensure you pass your wealth plan on to your family.

1. **Review this playbook.** This book is a great start, and I promise you'll find something new every time you reread it. Read this book at least once a year until you have mastered all of the principles.

2. **Write a purpose statement for your trust or will.** Initially, it's for you and what you want to create with your multigenerational wealth, but it is going to become the backbone of educating your heirs on what you want to see perpetuated when you leave this world. I've included a template copy of a purpose statement with the bonus materials for this book at https://get.biggerpockets.com/whitney/.

3. **If you have children, start their education now by giving them books and games that teach them about money, creating wealth, and the money principles you wish you knew growing up.** Their

age doesn't matter—two years, twenty years, thirty years old. We started playing games like *Cashflow for Kids*, *Monopoly*, *Catan*, and *7 Wonders* with our daughter at age four so she could learn concepts like assets, liabilities, cash flow, and value creation. We started reading *The Richest Man in Babylon* with my daughter when she was six as a storybook.

4. **Create a value economy within your household.** A lot of people pay for chores, but you can go beyond that. Move past the mentality of trading time for money (making your bed is a given, isn't it?), but instead start teaching your children about how they can create value at home. That lesson will translate into them understanding that the most important way to create wealth is by creating value. At age eight, our daughter started working alongside us on our real estate properties beyond just paperwork. With the income she's earned, she is learning to not only contribute to her community but also invest alongside us in our deals to learn about growing her wealth passively.

5. **Give your kids space to learn and (maybe) fail.** If you have kids, you must put them in a position where they can learn the principles in this book and even fail with their money choices. Right now, I would rather my daughter fail with $100 or $1,000 now than $10,000 or $100,000 in the future. One day, your children will be the heirs of your estate, so help them learn how to make good choices now, and, more importantly, how to learn from their mistakes while you are here to guide them.

6. **Record your journey.** Create a blog, create a website. Heck, you can even write a book like this! Keep it not only for yourself so you can solidify the knowledge you have, but also pass it along someday. My company is named AshWealth.com—A.S.H. are my daughter's initials. The business is hers when she is ready to take over.

These six steps are action items you can start working on right now that can change the trajectory of your life and the future of your family. It's never too late to start making changes, even if you feel like you are very behind.

Right now, the American population—and dare I say, most of the *world*—is facing a lack of financial capability,[21] which I believe is one of

---

21 Sicong Sun and Yu-Chih Chen, "Is Financial Capability a Determinant of Health? Theory and Evidence," *Journal of Family and Economic Issues* 43, no. 4 (November 2022): 744–755, https://www.ncbi.nlm.nih.gov/pmc/articles/PMC9628498/.

the greatest public crises. Again, financial incapability is a lack of putting one's financial knowledge into consistent and persistent action. We see it all the time, all over the world. That's why I started my coaching and mentoring business and AshWealth.com.

There are plenty of financial literacy materials available now, but most investors are still lost on how to create wealth for themselves, how to keep it, how to grow it, and how to ensure that their wealth is passed along to the next generation of their families. It's something we should all be heavily invested in, and the fact you're reading this book tells me you're ready to take the next step, even if it might not feel that way right now.

It's scary, I know—to think of taking calculated risks, doing the legwork to build the best team and find investments suited for you, even decluttering your life and expenses and basically thinking about things beyond *just your life*. But it's worth it.

I know for me, every time I look at my daughter's face I feel a sense of joy and pride. It's not just because I'm able to provide for all her needs *and* wants now because I put myself in a position to create wealth (outside of paycheck dependence), but also because I know I've *taught* her what she needs to make herself wealthy too. And that's the kind of feeling I want you to have after you've started applying what you read in this book.

═ YOUR CHAPTER ACTION PLAN ═

1. Review the principles in this book with your family and/or potential heirs on a regular basis until you have implemented all the steps and mastered all principles .
2. Write a purpose statement for your will or trust. This is another great chance to communicate to your heirs not only your final wishes, but also how you created your wealth and what they should do to carry on your legacy.
3. If you have kids in your life, be the transitional character in your family, and work to pass on your knowledge to them and help break the financial incapability cycle.
4. Record your journey and share it.

Real Stories of Money for Tomorrow
PRINCIPLES IN ACTION

Annie Dickerson, cofounder, Goodegg Investments

I remember the first time the light bulb went off for me in regard to taking control of my own financial future. I was working my ninth job in ten years. I was convinced something was wrong with me, because I kept going from job to job, trying to maximize my impact but always running into barriers with management, bureaucracy, and red tape. On top of that, I had two toddlers at home, and I was *exhausted*.

Knowing there had to be a better way to earn a living and provide for my family, I started to learn about the power of passive income. As I dug in, I suddenly realized that real estate just might be my ticket out of the W-2 game. I quickly did some back-of-the-napkin math and realized that if I could invest in ten small multifamily rental properties each generating $800 to $1,000 per month, I could replace my salary and never have to work again. Eureka!

I spent the next few months obsessively researching and learning how to quickly build up a portfolio of rental properties. But I ran into my next obstacle: Cash flow didn't exist in my home market of the San Francisco Bay Area. Not only that, but homes there tend to be very expensive, and the rental rates are typically not high enough to cover the high mortgage payments (not to mention the hurdles of rent control and strict tenant rights).

So the question begged: How could I invest outside of my home market to hit my cash flow numbers?

I knew very little about long-distance rental investing. But pretty soon I had a fourplex in Huntsville, Alabama. Everything went along swimmingly for the first few months. I thought I had become an instant real estate investing pro. I was quite full of myself, thinking I had figured it all out.

That's when everything came crashing down all at once.

That summer, I received a call from my property manager: "Are you sitting down?" (This is something you never want to hear from your property manager.)

She proceeded to tell me that the tenant whom we were going to evict the next day, for failure to pay her rent for the past several months, had left. But before she did, she stopped up all the sinks and tubs in her unit and turned the water on full blast. By the time anyone found out, the tenant had flooded not just her unit, but the one next door to that *and* the one next door to that.

Three of the four units in that fourplex sustained severe water damage and had to remain vacant that entire summer due to repairs. There went all my cash flow. Suddenly, instead of the property paying me, I had to start infusing more cash into the property, not to mention hours of my time going back and forth with the insurance company.

Then came my second light bulb moment.

I was ready to throw in the towel with this whole real estate investing thing. Between the calls with the insurance company, the theft and vandalism we'd experienced, and the unpredictable cash flow, I was no longer sure that it was all worth it—but that's when I remembered that long-distance rental properties weren't the only way to invest in real estate. There are so many different ways to invest in real estate, from active to passive investing, and from solo to group investing.

It wasn't that rental properties weren't right for me; they just weren't right for me at that stage of my life, with two young kids in tow and a new business venture that took up a huge chunk of mindshare and attention.

Since then, I have sold off all of the rental properties I acquired and have reinvested the capital into real estate syndications, where I can have a much more passive role while still reaping all the benefits of investing in real estate, including cash flow, equity, appreciation, and tax benefits.

Now, rather than a small portfolio of rental properties where I call all the shots but also have all the responsibility, my capital is spread out across thousands of doors of commercial multifamily, self-storage, industrial, and hospitality investments, in which I'm a passive investor. This allows me to diversify and expand my portfolio across a variety of markets, asset classes, operators, and business plans, while at the same time limiting my personal exposure and time commitment.

Because I've found a path for investing in real estate that works with my lifestyle and current phase of life, I'm able to grow my wealth while also being there for the moments with my family that truly matter. Best of all, because my husband and I are often talking about our various real estate investments with our kids, whether around the dinner table or in the car, they know more about real estate investing than I did in my early thirties.

In fact, my older son, who's now ten years old, recently asked if he could invest alongside my husband and me in a syndication we are investing in. Excited about this learning opportunity, I proceeded to open up the investment summary to tell him all about the deal, to which he responded, "Yeah, yeah, I know all of that already." He then proceeded to tell *me* all about the deal, based on everything he'd picked up from the various conversations around the house that my husband and I had engaged in about the opportunity. I was floored.

When I started out on this real estate investing journey, I was only thinking about myself and my own goal to quit my job. I thought that maybe if I were to build up a small portfolio of rental properties, I could eventually pass those along to my kids someday. I had no idea the wild ride that real estate would take me on.

The wealth that I've been able to accumulate in just a few short years has far surpassed anything I could have imagined. I've been able to build wealth in the traditional sense of the word, through net worth and assets, but perhaps even more important than that, I've been able to build wealth in the sense of being able to share these life-changing strategies with my children, so they can truly follow their passions and create a meaningful and intentional life by design. And even if all my investments were to completely tank, it will have been worth it for the valuable lessons I've been able to teach my kids about investing, finances, and entrepreneurship.

To me, that's true multigenerational wealth.

Conclusion

You deserve the world—you just have to earn it.

In the preceding pages, I've compiled everything you need to give yourself and your family the best start to fight the financial illiteracy and incapability epidemic and turn the tide of wealth creation in your favor. Because the truth is that where you start doesn't matter as much as where you end up. I've told you stories—my own, and those of other wealth-building gurus—of how just simple, targeted actions can get you to where you want to be.

I think that's what makes *Money for Tomorrow* so great. I'm not asking you to move mountains, take insane investment risks, or deprive yourself of happiness as you *hopefully* squirrel away enough money from your day job to retire comfortably. In fact, with the knowledge contained in this book, you'll be able to confidently plan the life you want for yourself. There will be no guesswork. You won't have to rely on hope or worry about stock market volatility or what laws the government may pass that will affect you in your golden years.

I'm helping you win the multigenerational wealth game by utilizing the three critical elements mentioned in the introduction.

Knowing Your Objective

This goal should be your primary one, the North Star guiding you toward a state where your passive income covers all of your desired living expenses. We covered this when it came time for you to choose your goals. Your objective should be that big moment when you have the freedom to do what you want and when you want, without having to consider financial constraints. More than that, this objective won't only help you—you'll be able to pass it on to future generations.

Understanding the Rules
Every game has its own set of rules that you have to live by, and the multigenerational wealth game is no different. In order to navigate it successfully, you need to know these rules like the back of your hand. We distilled these rules into four principles throughout this book: creating wealth, preserving wealth, nurturing wealth's growth, and ensuring the seamless passage of wealth to the next generation.

Playing the Game Successfully
When you combine your objectives with the rules, you have all you need to create success. Think of them as tactical moves on a game board— your financial decisions, your investments, and your wealth management techniques. What you have within these pages works outside of the traditional American dream we've been sold. It works to give you more control of your financial picture today as well as your retirement, with innovative ways to move from working for your money to having it work for you, discovering ways to invest and protect your investment even if you think we're on the brink of a recession or runaway inflation, as well as ways to lower your tax burden to help you keep more of your hard-earned money and accelerate its growth.

These are the tools that will help you navigate the journey from financial stability to multigenerational prosperity. We covered how to build a proper foundation for wealth by:
- Discovering what being wealthy *really* means, not what we've been conditioned to think it should look like.
- Using the secret framework every successful investor uses to choose their goals as well as achieve them, and the importance of passing this framework along to your heirs.

Then we took a deep dive into how to actually create wealth once you've figured out the foundation—what it means to be truly wealthy, and the goals you should set for yourself—by:
- Uncovering the wealth formula that will move from trading your time for dollars to becoming an investor who makes their money

from residual income—your money works, so you don't have to.
- Demystifying value-based spending and focusing on creating a budget that works for you by plugging money leaks, and finding out what you truly value to create the right motivation for your wealth build.

Next, we discussed how to *keep* the wealth—one of the more difficult parts of creating multigenerational wealth—by:
- Peeling back the curtain on how millionaires really spend their money, and what we can learn from them to help us on our quest to create wealth that spans multiple generations.
- Discussing how to build your own "moat" to protect your wealth—including three accounts that you must have—as well as demystifying the credit score.
- Understanding the four horsemen that can be like tiny landmines in your portfolio, waiting to blow up and create a disaster if you're not careful.

The next step in our plan involved learning how to grow the wealth we've managed to keep, by:
- Looking at what the path to becoming a millionaire really looks like; designing your dream life and how to make it a reality; as well as three assets that you can invest in on your journey.
- Breaking down the seven principles that govern conservative investing—four tenets and three amplifiers—that will help your investments to thrive in any market.
- Understanding the investing concepts that will make you wealthy: being able to understand how your assets are performing, the opportunity cost of not making a particular investment, and the power of the zero-percent tax bracket.

After the chapters on how to build the foundation for wealth, create wealth, keep wealth, and grow wealth, it was time for the section of the book that might have been the hardest for me to write, because it discusses something that we don't like being reminded of: our own mortality. But not planning for our passing doesn't absolve our family of the grief, stress, and confusion that happens when it comes time to deal with your estate.

In fact, *this* is where most families lose hundreds of thousands of dollars—maybe even millions if we account for the compounding effect of investments. In the last section of *Money for Tomorrow,* we covered how to ensure your wealth makes it to the next generation by:

- Creating your "I Love You Plan" that will make life easier for whoever you appoint as your executor/executrix or trustee, as well as ensure that grief is the most important thing for your family—not struggling to locate your important documents, interpreting your final wishes, or divvying up your estate.
- Finding and identifying the important individuals in your life who will act as your "advisory board" when it comes to helping you make the big decisions in your life, including the ones you make relating to your final wishes.

The last two chapters of this book were the most important. If you remember nothing else, I want you to remember the lessons in those chapters so you don't fail at passing wealth on. I told you the story of the two sons—both the children of a father who was relatively successful financially—but neither of them was able to replicate his success because they didn't know what he did.

You know what the craziest part of that story is? We recently discovered some handwritten diaries from Grandfather #2 (my dad's father) dated March 22, 1999, and in them, there was a brief section where he wrote about his mindset, his *why,* and how he built his estate—it was valuable information that could have completely changed the trajectory of both of his sons' lives as well as their families. However, for some reason, he never shared this information with his sons, and these ninety pages were found in 2023, buried under piles of unmarked documents and not set aside with the important things like his will.

Now that you've read this book, you won't make the same mistake.

Creating generational wealth isn't easy. But the process is simple … and it's worth it. Not only do you need to educate yourself, but you need to train the next generation to be the stewards of wealth too. You have everything you need to make your dream life a reality. All that's left is for you to go out and do it!

Will you?

Join the movement and supercharge your journey at AshWealth.com.

About the Author

Whitney Elkins-Hutten is the founder of financial and investing educational firm AshWealth.com, the director of investor education at private equity firm PassiveInvesting.com, coauthor of the international No. 1 bestseller *Resilient Women in Life and Business*, host of the *Passive Investing Made Simple* YouTube and *Multifamily Investor Nation* shows and podcasts, a real estate investor, personal finance trainer, wife, and mom.

After purchasing her first rental in 2002 and hitting a home run, then nearly losing it all on her second deal, Whitney took control and figured out how to invest the right way. Leveraging her background in scientific research and business operations, she replicated the very personal-finance and wealth-creation strategies the wealthy use in order to create financial freedom for herself and her family.

Whitney also had the unfortunate experience of settling five family estates with losses totaling over $700,000 in today's dollars due to poor financial education and planning—and 95 percent of those losses were completely avoidable. What is even more devastating, these losses compounded over thirty years mean a $5.3 million net loss to the next generation alone.

Motivated by this experience, Whitney founded AshWealth.com, where her mission is to reverse this trend of financial illiteracy and incapability. In the Investor Accelerator programs, Whitney helps families implement sound financial principles and wealth planning today in order to invest for passive income and long-term wealth for generations to come.

Today, Whitney is a partner in over $800 million of real estate assets, including more than 6,500 residential units (single-family, short-term, multifamily, and more) and over 2,200 self-storage units, and has flipped over $5 million in residential real estate. Whitney has been featured on more than ninety podcasts, including the *BiggerPockets Real Estate Podcast, BiggerPockets Rookie Podcast,* and *The Real Estate InvestHer Show.* She has spoken at the BiggerPockets conference, the Multifamily Investor Nation conference, BestEver Conference, The ONE Thing Couples Goal Setting Retreat, and InvestHer Con. Whitney is also a regular contributor to the BiggerPockets blog.

Whitney enjoys trail running in the foothills of Boulder, Colorado, as well as traveling, photography, craft beer, and playing board games with family and friends.

Join Whitney in the Investor Accelerator at AshWealth.com.

Acknowledgements

I would like to take a moment to thank all of the people who believed in this book idea and supported me every step of the way. Without your support, *Money for Tomorrow* would still just be an idea.

To my husband, Colin, thank you for being my rock and an amazing dad and chef, and for making sure that I was always well supplied with spicy chai while I worked on this book.

To my daughter, Avery, this book was always a passing thought until you came into the world. You always push me to be a better version of myself. Once in a while, you get shown the light, in the strangest of places, if you look at it right. You are my light.

To my parents, I wish you could be here to celebrate with me. The trials and tribulations you both went through I would never wish on anyone. But I'm thankful for all the wisdom I've gained from our journey together. You taught me one of the most important lessons—I am in full control of how I respond to the world and that life truly happens for you, not to you. I'm a better woman because of you two.

Thank you to my in-laws, not only for raising an amazing son, but for keeping me loved, grounded, and not letting me take myself too seriously. I can always count on you all for love, good food, and laughter when we're together.

Thank you to all my cousins, uncles, and aunts for loving and supporting me. It's easy to take for granted, but we have a pretty cool family, don't we?

Thank you to Devonnie Asher for taking my hours of videos, podcasts, and presentations and turning them into such a timeless classic. I hope you know just how impactful this work will be to the world, and you are a part of that!

Thank you to my clients and tribe for your support and feedback, and for allowing me the honor to serve you.

To Scott Trench, thank you for giving me my first shot at being a BiggerPockets writer. To Katie Miller, Savannah Wood, and the Bigger-Pockets team, thank you for believing in this book idea and being there every step of the way.

Thank you to Dan Handford, Danny Randazzo, Annie Dickerson, and Julie Lam for seeing in me what I had yet to see in myself, and giving me the opportunity to realize my potential.

Thank you to all my past coaches for your inspiration and for challenging me to think deeply and grow: Rich Fettke, Ryan Lee, Chris Miles, and Trevor McGregor. And thank you to all of those mentors whom I've never personally met, but follow oh so closely: Tony Robbins, Jay Papasan, Tom Bilyeu, and Dr. Mindy Pelz. We truly stand on the shoulders of giants.

Once in a while,
You get shown the light
In the strangest of places
If you look at it right.
—The Grateful Dead

References

Dennis, Elizabeth. "Women and Wealth: A Story of Evolution."
Morgan Stanley. June 8, 2022. https://www.morganstanley.com/
articles/female-invest-women-and-wealth.

DiGiulio, Sarah. "What is 'Swedish death cleaning' and should you be
doing it?" NBC News BETTER. November 7, 2017. https://www.
nbcnews.com/better/health/what-swedish-death-cleaning-
should-you-be-doing-it-ncna816511.

Elkins-Hutten, Whitney. "Millionaire Spending Habits to
Master—No Matter Your Income." *Personal Finance* (blog).
BiggerPockets. November 7, 2020. https://www.biggerpockets.
com/blog/key-millionaire-spending-habits.

"Form 5500 Search." EFAST2. U.S. Department of Labor. Accessed
July 4, 2023. https://www.efast.dol.gov/5500search/.

Gamburg, Ariel. "How to Legally Minimize Your Tax Expenses to
Increase Your Bottom Line." *Forbes*. September 4, 2018. https://
www.forbes.com/sites/forbesnycouncil/2018/09/14/how-to-
legally-minimize-your-tax-expenses-to-increase-your-bottom-
line.

"Generational Wealth: Why Do 70% of Families Lose Their Wealth in
the 2nd Generation?" Nasdaq. October 19, 2018. https://www.
nasdaq.com/articles/generational-wealth%3A-why-do-70-of-
families-lose-their-wealth-in-the-2nd-generation-2018-10.

Dickler, Jessica. "Boomers have more wealth 'than any other generation,' but millenials may not inherit as much as they hope." CNBC. Dec 9, 2022. https://www.cnbc.com/2022/12/09/great-wealth-transfer-why-millennials-may-inherit-less-than-expected.html.

Gunderson, Garrett. "How to Use the Cash Flow Index to Quickly and Safely Eliminate Your Debt." Wealth Factory. Accessed July 4, 2023. https://wealthfactory.com/articles/use-cash-flow-index-quickly-safely-eliminate-debt/.

Lakhiani, Vishen, and Irina Yugay. "The New Problem with Goal Setting and What You Can Do Instead: The 3 Most Important Questions." *Mindvalley* (blog). May 20, 2022. https://blog.mindvalley.com/3miqs/.

Lee, Ryan. "Our Story." Cashflow Tactics. Accessed July 4, 2023. https://cashflowtactics.com/our-story/.

McKnight, David. *The Power of Zero: How to Get to the 0% Tax Bracket and Transform Your Retirement.* Revised ed. New York: Crown, 2018.

Miles, Chris. "Money Ripples." Accessed July 4, 2023. https://money-ripples.com/.

Pino, Ivana. "57% of Americans can't afford a $1,000 emergency expense, says new report." *Fortune.* January 25, 2023. https://fortune.com/recommends/banking/57-percent-of-americans-cant-afford-a-1000-emergency-expense/.

Robbins, Tony. *MONEY: Master the Game: 7 Simple Steps to Financial Freedom.* New York: Simon & Schuster, 2014.

Robbins, Tony. "Unleash the Power Within." Virtual Seminar. 2021.

Sun, Sicong, and Yu-Chih Chen. "If Financial Capability a Determinant of Health? Theory and Evidence." *Journal of Family and Economic Issues* 43, no. 4 (November 2022): 744–755. https://www.ncbi.nlm.nih.gov/pmc/articles/PMC9628498/.

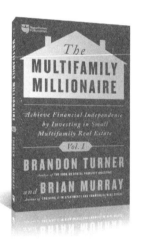

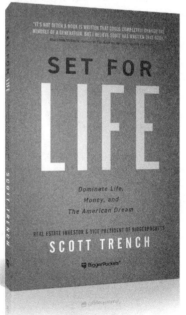

Short-Term Rental, Long-Term Wealth: Your Guide to Analyzing, Buying, and Managing Vacation Properties by Avery Carl

From analyzing potential properties to effectively managing your listings, this book is your one-stop resource for making a profit with STRs.

www.biggerpockets.com/strbook

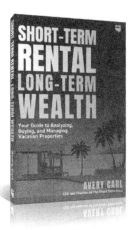

Start with Strategy: Craft Your Personal Real Estate Portfolio for Lasting Financial Freedom by David Meyer

Simplify your real estate goals with a portfolio plan that fits your personal values, resources, and skills.

https://store.biggerpockets.com/ start-with-strategy

Pillars of Wealth: How to Make, Save, and Invest Your Money to Achieve Financial Freedom by David Greene

Take the guesswork out of financial freedom with a strategy perfected by countless self-made millionaires.

www.biggerpockets.com/pillars

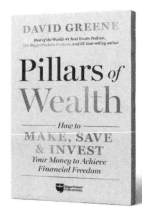

Looking for more?
Join the BiggerPockets Community

BiggerPockets brings together education, tools, and a community of more than 2+ million like-minded members—all in one place. Learn about investment strategies, analyze properties, connect with investor-friendly agents, and more.

Go to **biggerpockets.com** to learn more!

 Listen to a **BiggerPockets Podcast**

 Watch **BiggerPockets on YouTube**

 Join the **Community Forum**

 Learn more on **the Blog**

 Read more **BiggerPockets Books**

 Learn about our **Real Estate Investing Bootcamps**

 Connect with an **Investor-Friendly Real Estate Agent**

 Go Pro! Start, scale, and manage your portfolio with your **Pro Membership**

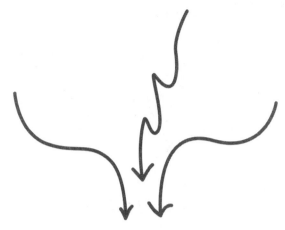

Follow us on social media!